fast, fresh, simple.

photography by william meppem

fast, fresh, simple.
Copyright © Donna Hay 2010. Design copyright © Donna Hay 2010
Photographs copyright © William Meppem 2010
Styling: Donna Hay
Art direction and design: Genevieve McKelvey and Hayley Incoll
Copy Editors: Kirsty McKenzie and Melanie Hansche
Recipe testing: Peta Dent and Siobhan Boyle

Reproduction by Graphic Print Group, South Australia
Produced in Hong Kong by Phoenix Offset on 157gsm Chinese Matt Art
Printed in China
10 11 12   5 4 3 2 1

fourth estate
An imprint of HarperCollins*Publishers*

First published in Australia and New Zealand in 2010, by Fourth Estate,
an imprint of HarperCollins*Publishers*

HarperCollins*Publishers* Australia Pty Limited, 25 Ryde Road,
Pymble, Sydney, NSW 2073, Australia
ABN 36 009 913 517
HarperCollins*Publishers*, 31 View Road, Glenfield, Auckland 10, New Zealand

national library of australia cataloguing-in-publication data
Hay, Donna. Fast, fresh, simple / Donna Hay. ISBN: 9780732291921 (pbk.)
Includes index. Cooking. Quick and easy cooking. 641.5

on the cover
summer tomato pasta, page 130
the new caesar salad, page 69
cheat's chocolate fondant, page 118

donna hay

fast, fresh, simple.

160+ fast recipes, fresh flavours and simple standbys for every day and any occasion

contents

*Ingredients marked with an asterisk have a glossary entry.

introduction

This book captures my philosophy on food and cooking in three easy words – *fast, fresh, simple*. That's *fast* quick-fix solutions for busy weeknights. *Fresh* flavours that offer a new spin on old favourites without the time-consuming preparation. And *simple* meal ideas using a mix of store-bought and fresh ingredients to create easy standbys for every day. I'm sure it's a mantra that most of us with a hectic work, family and social life can appreciate.

Like most busy people, I don't have hours to spare on preparation or complex presentation, time that I'd much rather spend with family and friends. So it's safe to say I've found just about every short cut around. It's in these pages that I share my secrets. I show you how to get all the flavour without the fuss to create dishes that look and taste good and give you more time to do the things you love.

In many ways this book is a culmination of another constant in my career: the pursuit of freshness, flavour and elegant simplicity (up there with my pursuit of the perfect ice-cream!). I've also included simple styling and decorating ideas in the last chapter to help bring your tabletop to life and frame your culinary creations. I hope it helps you rediscover cooking and entertaining as the wonderful, relaxing shared adventure it's meant to be. Happy cooking!

fast

These are my simple dinner solutions for those who need to deliver big results in a small amount of time. (It's my tribute to time-poor people everywhere!) Home at six and dinner on the table at six-thirty? No problem, these recipes will save the day. Whether it's a speedy pasta or a ready-made staple with a twist, you'll find all your weeknight wonders here.

fast

savoury

chorizo, spinach and ricotta frittata

Just because it's a fast recipe doesn't mean it has to be light on flavour.

simple three-cheese pasta

chorizo, spinach and ricotta frittata

2 chorizo*, sliced
1 tablespoon sage leaves
80g baby spinach leaves
4 eggs, lightly beaten
1 cup (250ml) single (pouring) cream*
sea salt and cracked black pepper
150g ricotta
buttered toast, to serve

Heat a 22cm non-stick frying pan over medium-high heat. Add the chorizo and sage and cook for 4–5 minutes or until chorizo is golden and crisp. Add the spinach and toss until wilted. Whisk together the eggs, cream, salt and pepper and pour into the pan. Place spoonfuls of ricotta around the pan, reduce heat to low and cook for 3 minutes. Place the frittata under a preheated hot grill and cook for 2 minutes or until frittata is just set and golden. Serve with thick slices of hot buttered toast. *Serves 2.*

simple three-cheese pasta

200g rigatoni or fettuccine
20g butter
2 teaspoons olive oil
1 tablespoon sage leaves
150g ricotta
⅓ cup (25g) finely grated parmesan
100g blue cheese, crumbled
sea salt and cracked black pepper

Cook the pasta in a large saucepan of boiling salted water for 10–12 minutes or until al dente. Drain and return to the pan to keep warm. Heat a small frying pan over medium-high heat. Add the butter and oil and cook until melted. Add the sage and cook for 3 minutes each side or until crisp, remove from heat and set aside. Toss the ricotta, parmesan and blue cheese through the pasta. Divide between serving plates and top with the sage and a little of the sage butter. Sprinkle with salt and pepper to serve. *Serves 2.*

I'm returning the sun-dried tomato to my repertoire... especially when a recipe needs an intense tomato hit.

rustic summer crumb pasta

garlic chickpeas and chorizo

rustic summer crumb pasta

200g spaghetti
100g sourdough or crusty bread
8 sun-dried tomato halves
2 cloves garlic, crushed
sea salt and cracked black pepper
1½ tablespoons olive oil
⅓ cup small basil leaves
1 small buffalo mozzarella*, halved
2 tablespoons balsamic vinegar
extra olive oil and finely grated parmesan, to serve

Cook the pasta in a large saucepan of boiling salted water for 8–10 minutes or until al dente. Drain and return to the pan to keep warm. While the pasta is cooking, place the bread, tomato, garlic, salt, pepper and oil in the bowl of a food processor and process in short bursts until the mixture resembles small crumbs. Heat a frying pan over medium-high heat. Add the crumb mixture and cook, stirring, for 4–5 minutes or until crumbs are golden. Toss the crumbs and basil with the pasta. Divide between serving bowls and top with the mozzarella. Drizzle with balsamic vinegar and extra olive oil. Sprinkle with parmesan. *Serves 2.*

garlic chickpeas and chorizo

3 chorizo*, sliced
4 cloves garlic, sliced
1 tablespoon shredded lemon zest
250g cherry tomatoes
1 x 400g can chickpeas (garbanzos), drained
⅓ cup basil leaves
1 tablespoon lemon juice
finely grated parmesan, to serve

Heat a non-stick frying pan over medium-high heat. Add the chorizo and cook for 3 minutes each side or until the chorizo is golden and crisp. Add the garlic and lemon zest and cook for 1 minute. Place the tomatoes in a sieve and press to split and release some of the excess juice and the seeds. Add the tomatoes and chickpeas to the pan and cook, stirring, for 3 minutes or until heated through. Stir through the basil and lemon juice. Divide between serving bowls and sprinkle with parmesan to serve. *Serves 2.*

barbecued lamb, eggplant and haloumi

2 tablespoons olive oil
2 teaspoons honey
2 cloves garlic, crushed
1 teaspoon chopped oregano leaves
sea salt and cracked black pepper
4 x 100g lamb leg or rump steaks
2 baby eggplant (aubergine), halved
150g haloumi*, cut into 4 slices
1 lemon, halved
50g rocket (arugula) leaves
olive oil, for drizzling
store-bought tzatziki* and char-grilled bread, to serve

Preheat a barbecue or char-grill pan over medium-high heat. Combine the oil, honey, garlic, oregano, salt and pepper and brush over the lamb, eggplant and haloumi. Cook the lamb, eggplant and haloumi on the barbecue or char-grill with the lemon, flesh-side down, for 3 minutes each side or until lamb is cooked to your liking, eggplant is tender and haloumi is golden. Divide between serving plates with the rocket leaves and serve with a squeeze of the grilled lemon, a drizzle of olive oil, the tzatziki and char-grilled bread. *Serves 2.*

I love an 'all on the bbq' recipe. Even the lemon benefits, its juice turning into a caramelised dressing.

barbecued lamb, eggplant and haloumi

chinese simmered pork

maple-glazed chicken

grilled chicken with caramelised balsamic tomatoes

maple-glazed chicken

¼ cup (60ml) maple syrup
¼ cup (60ml) water
½ teaspoon dried chilli flakes
½ teaspoon sea salt flakes
½ teaspoon cracked black pepper
2 x 200g chicken breast fillets, trimmed
roasted parsnips and steamed sugar snap peas, to serve

Place the maple syrup, water, chilli, salt and pepper in a non-stick
frying pan over medium heat. Bring to a simmer and add the chicken.
Cook for 4–5 minutes each side or until chicken is cooked through.
Serve the chicken with the pan sauce, roasted parsnips and steamed
sugar snap peas. *Serves 2.*

There's no need to mess with classic combinations, like pork with a sweet glaze or rocket with pear.

caramelised pork with pear and rocket salad

chinese simmered pork

⅓ cup (80ml) hoisin sauce*
¾ cup (180ml) Shaoxing* (Chinese rice wine) or dry sherry
¾ cup (180ml) chicken stock
1 teaspoon grated orange rind
2 teaspoons finely grated ginger
½ teaspoon Chinese five-spice*
1 x 400g pork fillet, trimmed and halved
steamed greens and jasmine rice, to serve

Place the hoisin, Shaoxing, stock, rind, ginger and five-spice in a non-stick frying pan over medium heat, bring to the boil and allow to simmer for 3 minutes. Add the pork and cook, covered, for 6 minutes each side or until pork is just cooked through. Remove from heat and rest the pork, covered, in the pan for 5 minutes. Remove the pork from the pan and slice. Serve with steamed greens, rice and the pan sauce. *Serves 2.*

Sticky hoisin and ginger are a perfect partner for juicy pork

grilled chicken with caramelised balsamic tomatoes

250g cherry tomatoes, halved
½ cup (125ml) balsamic vinegar
2 tablespoons sugar
1 tablespoon olive oil
2 cloves garlic, crushed
2 x 200g chicken breast fillets, trimmed
¼ cup basil leaves
8 baby bocconcini*
sea salt and cracked black pepper, to serve

Preheat oven to 200°C (400°F). Line a small baking tray with non-stick baking paper and add the tomato. Sprinkle with balsamic and sugar and bake for 25–30 minutes or until tomatoes are soft and caramelised. Combine the oil and garlic and brush over the chicken. Cook the chicken on a preheated barbecue or char-grill pan for 4–5 minutes each side or until cooked through. Place the chicken on serving plates and serve with the tomato, basil and bocconcini and sprinkle with salt and pepper. *Serves 2.*

caramelised pork with pear and rocket salad

2 x 235g pork cutlets, trimmed
olive oil, for brushing
sea salt and cracked black pepper
¼ cup (60ml) malt vinegar
2 tablespoons caster (superfine) sugar
1 large piece lemon rind
12 sage leaves
pear and rocket salad
1 firm brown pear, very thinly sliced
30g baby rocket (arugula) leaves
½ cup (40g) shaved parmesan
olive oil, for drizzling

Heat a frying pan over high heat. Brush the pork with oil and sprinkle with salt and pepper. Add the pork to the pan and cook for 2–3 minutes each side or until well browned. Set aside. Add the vinegar, sugar, lemon rind and sage to the pan and bring to the boil. Allow to rapidly simmer for 5 minutes or until thickened and slightly syrupy. Return the pork to the pan and cook for 3–4 minutes each side or until the pork is cooked to your liking. Combine the pear, rocket and parmesan and place on serving plates with the pork. Remove the lemon rind from the pan and spoon the sauce over the pork. Drizzle the salad with olive oil to serve. *Serves 2.*

standby porcini pasta

20g dried porcini mushrooms*
200g spaghetti
1½ tablespoons olive oil
2 cloves garlic, crushed
1 tablespoon thyme leaves
1 cup (70g) fresh breadcrumbs
sea salt and cracked black pepper
finely grated parmesan and olive oil, to serve

Place the porcini in a bowl, cover with boiling water and set aside. Cook the pasta in a large saucepan of boiling salted water for 8–10 minutes or until al dente. Drain and keep warm. Place the pan back on the heat. Add the oil, garlic and thyme and cook for 2 minutes. Drain the porcini and roughly chop. Add the porcini to the pan with the breadcrumbs and cook, stirring, for 4 minutes or until crumbs are golden. Add the pasta to the pan with salt and pepper and toss to coat. Divide between serving plates and sprinkle with parmesan and olive oil. *Serves 2.*

When I cook this recipe I'm amazed
by the fact that I can make such
a tasty meal from very little.

standby porcini pasta

To me, the perfect steak sandwich
is all about char-grilling the
bread as well as the steak.

char-grilled steak sandwiches

lentils with pancetta and olives

fig and gorgonzola tart

char-grilled steak sandwiches

4 x 80g 1cm-thick beef rump or topside steaks
4 thick slices bread
olive oil, for brushing
sea salt
salad leaves, to serve
cracked black pepper
¼ cup (75g) store-bought caramelised onion relish*
garlic mayonnaise
1 clove garlic, crushed
¼ cup (75g) store-bought whole-egg mayonnaise*

Preheat a barbecue or char-grill pan over medium-high heat. To make
the garlic mayonnaise, combine the garlic and mayonnaise and set
aside. Brush the steaks and bread with a little oil and sprinkle the
steaks with salt. Place on the barbecue or char-grill and cook for
1 minute each side or until the bread is toasted and the steak is cooked
to your liking. Place 2 slices of the bread on serving plates and spread
with the garlic mayonnaise. Top with the salad leaves, steak, pepper,
caramelised onion and remaining bread slices and serve. *Serves 2.*

lentils with pancetta and olives

8 slices pancetta*
2 teaspoons olive oil
2 cloves garlic, crushed
2 teaspoons oregano leaves
1 x 400g can lentils, drained and rinsed
½ cup (125ml) chicken stock
½ cup (60) pitted black olives
50g baby spinach leaves
sea salt and cracked black pepper
grated parmesan and lemon wedges, to serve

Heat a non-stick frying pan over high heat and cook the pancetta, in
batches, for 1 minute each side or until crisp. Remove from pan and set
aside. Add the oil, garlic and oregano to the pan and cook for 1 minute
or until fragrant. Add the lentils and stock and simmer for 5 minutes
or until the stock is absorbed. Stir in the olives, spinach, salt and
pepper. Divide the lentil mixture between shallow bowls and top with
the crispy pancetta. Sprinkle with parmesan and lemon juice. *Serves 2.*

fig and gorgonzola tart

2 x 200g sheets store-bought shortcrust pastry*, thawed
80g gorgonzola*
2 teaspoons oregano leaves
3 figs, quartered
1 tablespoon honey
1 tablespoon olive oil
cracked black pepper
50g watercress sprigs
6 slices prosciutto*

Preheat oven to 180°C (350°F). Cut pastry into 2 x 18cm rounds
and place on baking trays lined with non-stick baking paper.
Spread each pastry with gorgonzola and top with oregano and
figs. Place the honey, oil and pepper in a bowl and mix to combine.
Drizzle the tarts with half the honey mixture. Bake for 15 minutes
or until pastry is golden and crisp. To serve, top with watercress
and prosciutto and remaining olive oil and honey mixture. *Serves 2.*

Make smaller versions of this delicious tart to serve at your next drinks party or as a simple and elegant starter for a dinner party.

One of my new favourite combinations.
Crisp, molten haloumi with honey,
herbs and lemon.

chicken with haloumi and honey

pasta with ricotta and prosciutto

olive and almond couscous with oregano lamb

olive and almond couscous with oregano lamb

300g lamb backstrap (boneless loin)
olive oil, for brushing
1 tablespoon marjoram or oregano leaves
sea salt and cracked black pepper
olive and almond couscous
1 cup (200g) couscous*
1¼ cups (310ml) hot chicken stock
20g butter, softened
¼ cup (40g) sliced green olives
⅓ cup (20g) toasted flaked almonds

To make the olive and almond couscous, place the couscous in a bowl, pour over the stock and add the butter. Cover with plastic wrap and stand for 5 minutes or until the stock has been absorbed. Stir through the olives and almonds. Brush the lamb with oil. Combine the oregano, salt and pepper and press into the lamb. Heat a frying pan over medium-high heat and cook the lamb for 4 minutes each side or until cooked to your liking. Rest the lamb for 3 minutes, then slice. Place the couscous in bowls and top with the lamb to serve. *Serves 2.*

pasta with pistachios and mint

Versions of this recipe have been
one of the test kitchen's favourite
'special' lunches for years.

rocket pasta with seared tuna

chicken with haloumi and honey

2 x 200g chicken breast fillets, trimmed
150g haloumi*, cut into 4 slices
1 tablespoon shredded lemon zest
6 sprigs lemon thyme
1 tablespoon olive oil
1 tablespoon honey
fig and rocket (arugula) salad, to serve

Preheat oven to 180°C (350°F). Place the chicken, haloumi, zest and lemon thyme in a ceramic baking dish. Combine the oil and honey and pour over. Bake for 18–20 minutes or until chicken is cooked through. Serve with a fig and rocket salad. *Serves 2.*

pasta with ricotta and prosciutto

200g wide pasta or rigatoni
2 tablespoons olive oil
4 cloves garlic, sliced
sea salt and cracked black pepper
¾ cup (150g) ricotta
2 tablespoons basil leaves
6 slices prosciutto*, torn
finely grated parmesan, to serve

Cook the pasta in a large saucepan of boiling salted water for 8–10 minutes or until al dente. Drain and return to the pan to keep warm. Return the pan to the heat and add the oil, garlic, salt and pepper and cook for 1 minute. Return the pasta to the pan and toss to coat. Place pasta on serving plates and top with the ricotta, basil and prosciutto. Sprinkle with parmesan and serve. *Serves 2.*

I love a pasta that can be tossed together in a matter of minutes, no simmering sauce required.

pasta with pistachios and mint

200g penne
¾ cup (105g) shelled unsalted pistachios, toasted
1 clove garlic, crushed
⅓ cup finely shredded mint leaves
2 tablespoons olive oil
¼ cup (20g) finely grated parmesan
sea salt and cracked black pepper
extra finely grated parmesan, to serve

Cook the pasta in a large saucepan of boiling salted water for 8–10 minutes or until al dente. While the pasta is cooking, roughly chop the pistachios and mix with the garlic, mint, oil and parmesan. Toss the nut mixture with the cooked pasta and sprinkle with salt and pepper and extra parmesan to serve. *Serves 2.*

rocket pasta with seared tuna

200g spaghetti
1 x 125g tuna steak
olive oil, for brushing
sea salt and cracked black pepper
1 tablespoon olive oil, extra
2 tablespoons salted capers, rinsed
3 cloves garlic, sliced
pinch dried chilli flakes
50g finely shredded large rocket (arugula) leaves
2 tablespoons lemon juice
cracked black pepper and lemon wedges, to serve

Cook the pasta in a large saucepan of boiling salted water for 8–10 minutes or until al dente. While the pasta is cooking, heat a non-stick frying pan over high heat. Brush the tuna with oil and sprinkle with salt and pepper. Cook for 30 seconds to 1 minute each side or until seared. Remove from pan and set aside. Add the extra olive oil, capers, garlic and chilli to the pan and cook for 3 minutes or until the capers are crisp. Add the cooked pasta, rocket and lemon juice to the pan and toss to combine. Divide the pasta between serving bowls, slice the tuna and place on top of the pasta. Sprinkle with pepper and serve with lemon wedges. *Serves 2.*

thai chicken soup

I love this classic Thai combination of sweet, sour, spicy and salty.

sticky chilli chicken

thai chicken soup

3 cups (750ml) chicken stock
2 cups (500ml) coconut milk*
1 long red chilli*, thinly sliced
1 tablespoon grated ginger
6 kaffir lime leaves*, shredded
2 coriander (cilantro) roots, washed and finely chopped
1 x 200g chicken breast fillet, trimmed and sliced
60g snow peas (mange tout), shredded
1 tablespoon fish sauce*
1 tablespoon lime juice
coriander (cilantro) leaves and extra sliced chilli, to serve

Place stock, coconut milk, chilli, ginger, lime leaves and coriander root in a saucepan over medium-high heat and bring to the boil. Reduce heat and simmer for 3 minutes. Add the chicken and cook for 2 minutes. Add the snow peas and cook for a further minute. Stir though the fish sauce and lime juice. Ladle into bowls and serve with coriander leaves and extra chilli, if desired. *Serves 2.*

Kaffir lime leaves are one of my kitchen must-haves for an instant flavour rescue.

sticky chilli chicken

3 long red chillies*, deseeded and finely sliced
1 tablespoon finely grated ginger
1 stalk lemongrass, white part only, finely sliced
2 tablespoons fish sauce*
⅓ cup (80ml) white wine vinegar
⅓ cup (75g) caster (superfine) sugar
2 x 200g chicken breast fillets, trimmed and halved lengthways
300g snake or green beans, finely sliced
steamed rice, mint, basil and coriander (cilantro) leaves
   and lime wedges, to serve

Place the chilli, ginger, lemongrass, fish sauce, vinegar and sugar in a deep frying pan over high heat and cook for 5 minutes or until the mixture is reduced and thickened slightly. Add the chicken and cook for 4 minutes. Turn the chicken, add the beans and continue to cook for a further 3–4 minutes or until chicken is cooked through. Serve the chicken and beans with steamed rice, mint, basil and coriander leaves and lime wedges. *Serves 2.*

crispy chilli duck and noodle salad

20g cellophane (bean thread) noodles*
½ cup mint leaves
½ cup basil leaves
½ cup coriander (cilantro) leaves
2 tablespoons lime juice
1 teaspoon fish sauce*
1 teaspoon sugar
finely sliced long red chilli*, chilli sauce and lime wedges, to serve
crispy chilli duck
2 x 150g duck breast fillets, trimmed and sliced
1 tablespoon chilli powder
¼ cup (50g) rice flour*
sea salt and cracked black pepper
vegetable oil, for frying

Place the noodles in a bowl and cover with boiling water. Set aside for 8 minutes or until tender, drain. To make the crispy chilli duck, toss the duck in the combined chilli, flour, salt and pepper. Heat enough oil over high heat in a frying pan to shallow-fry. Add the duck and cook for 1 minute each side or until crisp and golden. Drain on absorbent paper. Toss the noodles with the mint, basil and coriander. Combine the juice, fish sauce and sugar and pour over the noodles. Top with the duck and serve with chilli, chilli sauce and lime wedges. *Serves 2.*

With its spicy flavour and crispy texture, this recipe is so addictive it should come with a warning.

crispy chilli duck and noodle salad

baked italian chicken

porcini salt minute steaks with rösti

herb and honey lamb cutlets

porcini salt minute steaks with rösti

15g dried porcini mushrooms*
1 tablespoon sea salt flakes
4 x 90g thin-cut beef fillet or sirloin steaks
olive oil, for brushing
rösti
1 large potato (380g), peeled and grated
1 tablespoon rosemary leaves
50g butter, melted
sea salt
vegetable oil, for frying

Place the porcini and salt in the bowl of a small food processor and process until mixture is a fine powder. Set aside. To make the rösti, place the potato, rosemary, butter and salt in a bowl and mix to combine. Heat a frying pan over medium-high heat. Add a little oil and a quarter of the potato mixture. Spread the mixture to a thin pancake. Cook for 3–4 minutes each side or until crisp. Repeat with remaining mixture and keep warm. Brush the steaks with oil and sprinkle with porcini salt. Heat a frying pan over high heat. Add the steaks and cook for 1 minute each side. Serve with extra porcini salt and rösti. *Serves 2.*

Creamy feta, rosemary, honey and lemon take the humble meatball to a whole new level.

greek-inspired lamb meatballs

baked italian chicken

250g cherry tomatoes, halved
120g piece flat pancetta*, coarsely chopped
2 tablespoons oregano leaves
8 cloves garlic
1 tablespoon olive oil
2 x 200g chicken breast fillets, trimmed
½ cup (80g) black olives
cracked black pepper
basil leaves and finely grated parmesan, to serve

Preheat oven to 200°C (400°F). Place the tomato, pancetta, oregano, garlic and oil in a baking dish and toss to combine. Bake for 25 minutes. Add the chicken and olives to the dish and sprinkle with pepper. Bake for 20 minutes or until the chicken is tender. Place on serving plates, top with basil and sprinkle with parmesan. *Serves 2.*

herb and honey lamb cutlets

4 x 75g double lamb cutlets
2 cloves garlic
½ cup mint leaves
½ cup flat-leaf parsley leaves
½ cup coriander (cilantro) leaves
¼ cup (60ml) red wine vinegar
2 tablespoons honey
sea salt and cracked black pepper

Trim the cutlets of excess fat and place in a non-metallic bowl. Place the garlic, mint, parsley, coriander, vinegar, honey, salt and pepper in the bowl of a food processor and process until finely chopped. Pour the marinade over the lamb and allow to stand for 10–15 minutes. Heat a non-stick frying pan over high heat. Remove lamb from marinade and cook lamb for 1 minute each side or until well browned. Reduce heat to low, add the marinade to the pan and cook for 4–6 minutes or until lamb is cooked to your liking and the marinade has thickened to a sticky sauce. Serve the lamb with steamed greens. *Serves 2.*

I like to use double lamb cutlets so you can get a golden crust on the outside without drying the meat.

greek-inspired lamb meatballs

⅓ cup (65g) couscous*
⅔ cup (160ml) chicken stock
300g lamb mince (ground lamb)
1 tablespoon honey
1 teaspoon finely grated lemon rind
1 teaspoon chopped rosemary leaves
sea salt and cracked black pepper
80g feta*, coarsely chopped
flatbread, hummus*, baby spinach leaves, mint leaves and halved
    cherry tomatoes, to serve

Place the couscous in a bowl and pour over the hot stock. Cover with plastic wrap and stand until the stock has been absorbed. Combine the couscous, mince, honey, rind, rosemary, salt and pepper and mix well. Stir in the feta. Shape the mixture into ⅓-cup flat patties. Heat a non-stick frying pan over medium heat. Add the patties and cook for 4–5 minutes each side or until cooked through. To serve, place flatbread on serving plates and spread with hummus. Top with spinach, mint, tomato and the meatballs. *Serves 2.*

ginger-poached tofu with noodles

2 cups (500ml) chicken or vegetable stock
2 tablespoons shredded ginger
1 stalk lemongrass, halved lengthways
¼ cup (60ml) soy sauce
1 star anise
300g firm silken tofu*, thickly sliced
400g fresh egg or udon noodles*
60g sugar snap peas, halved, or bok choy*

Place stock, ginger, lemongrass, soy and star anise in a deep frying pan over high heat and bring to the boil. Reduce heat and simmer for 3 minutes. Add the tofu and poach for 3 minutes each side, remove from pan and keep warm. Add the noodles and greens to the pan and cook for 3 minutes or until tender. Place the noodles and greens in bowls and top with the tofu. Spoon over a little of the poaching liquid to serve. *Serves 2.*

One of the best things about tofu
is its ability to soak up flavours.

ginger-poached tofu with noodles

This vibrantly flavoured salad
is my ultimate summer standby.

chicken rice noodle salad with coconut milk dressing

chinese soy chicken

bacon and lentil soup

chicken rice noodle salad with coconut milk dressing

150g flat rice noodles*
2 x 200g cooked chicken breast fillets, sliced
2 long red chillies*, deseeded and finely sliced
4 finely shredded kaffir lime leaves*
3 green onions (scallions), finely sliced
½ cup coriander (cilantro) leaves
½ cup mint leaves
½ cup basil leaves
coconut milk dressing
½ cup (125ml) coconut milk*
1 tablespoon fish sauce*
2 tablespoons lime juice
1 tablespoon caster (superfine) sugar

Place rice noodles in a large bowl, cover with boiling water and stand for 4–6 minutes or until soft. Drain and rinse. Toss the noodles with the chicken, chilli, lime leaf, onion, coriander, mint and basil. To make the coconut milk dressing, combine the coconut milk, fish sauce, juice and sugar. Pour over the salad to serve. Serves 2.

chinese soy chicken

2 tablespoons finely shredded ginger
½ cup (125ml) Shaoxing* (Chinese rice wine) or dry sherry
½ cup (125ml) chicken stock
2 tablespoons soy sauce
1 stick cinnamon
1 star anise
2 tablespoons brown sugar
2 x 200g chicken breast fillets, trimmed
6 small stalks gai larn (Chinese broccoli) or broccolini*, trimmed
steamed jasmine rice, to serve

Place the ginger, Shaoxing, stock, soy, cinnamon, star anise and sugar in a non-stick frying pan over high heat and bring to the boil. Reduce temperature and simmer for 4 minutes. Add the chicken and cook for 6 minutes. Turn the chicken and cook for a further 4 minutes. Add the gai larn, cover and cook for a further 2 minutes or until the chicken and gai larn are tender. Serve with rice. Serves 2.

This recipe is one of my 'oldies but goodies'. I never seem to tire of this flavour combination.

bacon and lentil soup

2 teaspoons vegetable oil
1 onion, finely chopped
2 rashers bacon, finely chopped
1 teaspoon thyme leaves
¾ cup (150g) red lentils
1.25 litres (5 cups) chicken stock
sea salt and cracked black pepper
finely grated parmesan and sour cream, to serve

Heat a saucepan over medium-high heat. Add the oil, onion and bacon and cook for 4 minutes or until lightly browned. Add the thyme, lentils and stock, cover and simmer for 20 minutes or until the lentils start to break down. Stir in salt and pepper. Ladle between bowls and top with parmesan and sour cream to serve. Serves 2.

The lentil base has a certain earthy nuttiness that makes this soup more complex than the few ingredients suggest. It's probably why I always have it on standby in my freezer.

I'm of the belief that for a salad
to be a meal it should have gusto.
This one has plenty of it.

roasted pumpkin and couscous salad

lemon, chicken and basil pasta

coriander and lime chicken tortillas

coriander and lime chicken tortillas

2 x 200g cooked chicken breast fillets, shredded
1 tablespoon lime juice
1 long green chilli*, finely sliced
sea salt and cracked black pepper
4 tortillas
sour cream, lime wedges and snipped chives, to serve
coriander and lime salsa
⅓ cup coriander (cilantro) leaves
1 tablespoon lime juice
½ avocado, chopped

To make the coriander and lime salsa, place the coriander, lime juice and avocado in a bowl and mix gently to combine. To make the chicken filling, combine the chicken, lime juice, chilli, salt and pepper. Heat a non-stick frying pan over medium heat. Add a tortilla to the pan and warm for 1 minute each side. Fill one half of the tortilla with the chicken mixture and top with the coriander and lime salsa. Fold over the tortilla to enclose the filling. Repeat with remaining tortillas and filling and serve with sour cream, chives and lime wedges. *Serves 2.*

chicken salad with cashews and mint

When I was young, I thought fish was a bit boring. Now, give me crispy-skin fish with a kick of harissa any day.

crispy harissa fish with lemon couscous

roasted pumpkin and couscous salad

16 thin slices pumpkin
1 tablespoon olive oil
1 cup (200g) couscous*
1¼ cups (310ml) hot chicken stock
1 tablespoon shredded preserved lemon rind*
¼ cup shredded mint leaves
200g firm feta*, sliced
honey-cumin dressing
1 tablespoon honey
½ teaspoon ground cumin
1 tablespoon olive oil
1 tablespoon white wine vinegar

Preheat oven to 200°C (400°F). Place the pumpkin on a baking tray lined with non-stick baking paper and brush with oil. Bake for 25 minutes or until golden. Place the couscous in a bowl and pour over the stock. Cover with plastic wrap and allow to stand for 5 minutes or until the stock has been absorbed. Stir the rind and mint through the couscous. To make the dressing, whisk together the honey, cumin, oil and vinegar. To serve, place the pumpkin, feta and couscous on serving plates and spoon over the dressing. *Serves 2.*

lemon, chicken and basil pasta

200g spaghetti
2 tablespoons lemon juice
2 tablespoons olive oil
⅓ cup (25g) finely grated parmesan cheese
1 x 200g cooked chicken breast fillet, shredded
½ cup shredded basil leaves
sea salt and cracked black pepper

Cook the pasta in a large saucepan of boiling salted water for 8–10 minutes or until al dente. Drain and return to the warm pan. While the pasta is cooking, place the juice, oil and parmesan in a bowl and whisk to combine. Add to the pasta with the chicken, basil, salt and pepper and toss to combine. Serve immediately. *Serves 2.*

chicken salad with cashews and mint

2 x 200g cooked chicken breast fillets, shredded
1 green mango*, peeled and shredded
1 cup (80g) shredded cabbage
1 cup small mint leaves
¾ cup (120g) roasted unsalted cashews
1 long green chilli*, finely sliced
lime dressing
2 tablespoons store-bought whole-egg mayonnaise*
⅓ cup (80ml) lime juice
1 tablespoon caster (superfine) sugar

Combine the chicken, mango, cabbage, mint and cashews in a bowl. Divide between serving plates. To make the dressing, combine the mayonnaise, juice and sugar. Spoon the dressing over the salad and top with the chilli. *Serves 2.*

crispy harissa fish with lemon couscous

1 tablespoon harissa*
2 x 175g firm white fish fillets, skin on
1 tablespoon olive oil
store-bought tzatziki* and lemon wedges, to serve
lemon couscous
2 teaspoons finely grated lemon rind
2 tablespoons lemon juice
1 cup (200g) couscous*
sea salt and cracked black pepper
1½ cups (375ml) hot chicken stock
100g baby spinach leaves

To make the lemon couscous, place the rind and juice, couscous, salt and pepper in bowl and mix to combine. Pour over the stock and cover with plastic wrap. Set aside until all the stock has been absorbed and stir through the spinach. To cook the fish, spread the harissa over the flesh side of the fish. Heat a non-stick frying pan over medium heat. Add the oil to the pan and the fish, skin-side down, and cook for 4–5 minutes or until the skin is crisp. Turn and cook for 1 minute or until fish is just cooked. Divide the couscous and fish between serving plates and serve with tzatziki and lemon wedges. *Serves 2.*

roman bean and grilled goat's cheese salad

This tasty pasta is guaranteed to turn anyone who's anti-sprout.

orecchietti with brussels sprouts and pancetta

roman bean and grilled goat's cheese salad

4 long slices baguette
100g firm goat's cheese, sliced
400g Roman (flat) beans, trimmed and blanched
50g curly endive (frisée) leaves
2 tablespoons sliced black olives
1 tablespoon olive oil
1 tablespoon red wine vinegar
½ teaspoon caster (superfine) sugar

Place the baguette on a baking tray and top with the goat's cheese. Place under a preheated hot grill and cook for 2–3 minutes or until the cheese is golden. Place beans and endive on serving plates. Combine the olives, oil, vinegar and sugar and spoon over the salad. Top with the goat's cheese baguette to serve. *Serves 2.*

Use this recipe for an elegant summer lunch or make smaller servings for a dinner party starter.

orecchietti with brussels sprouts and pancetta

300g small Brussels sprouts
200g orecchietti*
8 slices pancetta*
30g butter
1 clove garlic, crushed
2 teaspoons oregano leaves
⅔ cup (165ml) single (pouring) cream*
2 tablespoons lemon juice
finely grated parmesan, to serve

Remove the outer leaves from the sprouts and cut into quarters. Cook the pasta in a large saucepan of boiling salted water for 8–10 minutes or until al dente. Drain and return to the pan to keep warm. While the pasta is cooking, place the pancetta under a preheated hot grill and grill until well browned. Set aside. Heat a frying pan over medium-high heat. Add the butter, garlic and oregano to the pan and cook for 1 minute. Add the sprouts and cook for 3–4 minutes or until just soft. Add the cream, lemon juice and pasta and toss until warmed through. Crumble the pancetta into fine pieces. To serve, divide the pasta between bowls and top with the pancetta crumbs and parmesan. *Serves 2.*

lime and coconut poached fish

1 cup (250ml) coconut milk*
1 long green chilli*, finely sliced
¼ cup (60ml) lime juice
6 kaffir lime leaves*, finely shredded
1 tablespoon fish sauce
200g firm white fish fillets
½ cup coriander (cilantro) leaves
steamed jasmine rice and steamed greens, to serve

Place the coconut milk, chilli, juice, leaves and fish sauce in a frying pan over medium-low heat. Bring to the boil, reduce heat and simmer for 4 minutes. Add the fish and cook for 3–4 minutes each side or until tender. To serve, divide the fish and the poaching liquid between serving plates and sprinkle with coriander. Serve with steamed rice and greens. *Serves 2.*

This is what I cook on summer beach holidays. So when I cook it at home, my thoughts return to the beach.

lime and coconut poached fish

Wrap these cakes and their sides in flatbread for a mini portable feast.

sesame chicken cakes

salt and pepper chicken

sesame-crusted salmon with ponzu dressing

salt and pepper chicken

2 x 200g chicken breast fillets, trimmed
3 teaspoons Chinese five-spice*
1 teaspoon table salt
½ teaspoon cracked black pepper
½ teaspoon chilli powder
2 tablespoons rice flour*
vegetable oil, for shallow frying
steamed jasmine rice, sugar snap peas, lemon wedges and coriander
  (cilantro) leaves, to serve

Slice the chicken into thin flat pieces. Combine the five-spice, salt, pepper, chilli and flour. Sprinkle over the chicken and toss to coat. Heat 1cm of oil in a frying pan over high heat. Cook the chicken, in batches, for 1–2 minutes each side or until golden and cooked through. Serve the chicken with lemon wedges, coriander, steamed sugar snap peas and steamed jasmine rice. *Serves 2.*

zucchini, mint, haloumi and lemon salad

sesame chicken cakes

350g chicken mince (ground chicken)
¼ cup (15g) fresh breadcrumbs
2 tablespoons sweet chilli sauce
2 tablespoons finely chopped coriander (cilantro) leaves
sea salt
2 tablespoons sesame seeds
vegetable oil, for shallow frying
1 Lebanese cucumber, sliced with a vegetable peeler
1 stick celery, thinly sliced
¼ cup coriander (cilantro) leaves, extra
2 teaspoons rice wine vinegar*
1 tablespoon vegetable oil
extra sweet chilli sauce, to serve

Place the mince, breadcrumbs, chilli sauce, coriander and salt in a bowl and mix well to combine. Roll 2 tablespoons of the mixture into a flat cake. Sprinkle both sides of the cake with the sesame seeds and repeat with remaining mixture. Heat 1cm of oil in a frying pan over high heat. Add the cakes, in batches, and cook for 3–4 minutes each side or until golden and cooked through. Toss together the cucumber, celery, coriander, vinegar and oil. Place on serving plates and serve with the chicken cakes and extra sweet chilli sauce. *Serves 2.*

sesame-crusted salmon with ponzu dressing

2 x 180g salmon fillets, skin off
¼ cup (35g) black sesame seeds*
1 tablespoon vegetable oil
50g Asian salad leaves
ponzu dressing
2 tablespoons mirin*
1 tablespoon soy sauce
¼ cup (60ml) lime juice

To make the ponzu dressing, place the mirin, soy and lime juice in a saucepan over medium heat and bring to the boil. Remove from heat and set aside to cool. Press both sides of the salmon into the sesame seeds. Heat a frying pan over medium-high heat. Add the oil and the salmon and cook for 3–4 minutes each side or until cooked to your liking. Slice the salmon and arrange on plates with the salad leaves. Spoon over the ponzu dressing to serve. *Serves 2.*

zucchini, mint, haloumi and lemon salad

2 zucchini (courgette), coarsely grated
½ cup finely shredded mint leaves
50g baby spinach leaves
sea salt and cracked black pepper
2 tablespoons pomegranate molasses*
250g haloumi*, thickly sliced
olive oil, for brushing and drizzling
pinch dried chilli flakes
1 lemon, halved

Place the zucchini, mint, spinach, salt, pepper and pomegranate molasses in a bowl and toss gently to combine. Heat a non-stick frying pan over medium-high heat. Brush the haloumi with a little oil and sprinkle to taste with chilli. Place the haloumi and lemon, cut-side down, in the pan and cook the haloumi for 2 minutes each side or until golden and the lemon flesh has caramelised. To serve, divide the zucchini salad between plates and top with the haloumi. Drizzle with a little oil and squeeze over the caramelised lemon. *Serves 2.*

chicken and zucchini salad with preserved lemon dressing

2 zucchini (courgette), sliced with a vegetable peeler
2 x 200g cooked chicken breast fillets, shredded
½ cup mint leaves
sea salt and cracked black pepper
preserved lemon dressing
1 tablespoon olive oil
1 tablespoon lemon juice
1 teaspoon white sugar
1 tablespoon finely shredded preserved lemon rind*

Toss the zucchini with the chicken, mint, salt and pepper. To make the preserved lemon dressing, place the oil, juice and sugar in a bowl and stir to dissolve the sugar. Stir through the preserved lemon. To serve, place the zucchini and chicken mixture on plates. Spoon over the preserved lemon dressing. *Serves 2.*

I love the sour tang of preserved lemon, it adds instant flavour to a salad, couscous or pasta.

zucchini salad with chicken and preserved lemon dressing

fast
sweet

pavlova cups

raspberry trifle

pavlova cups

4 x 15g store-bought vanilla meringues
1 cup (250ml) single (pouring) cream*, whipped
250g strawberries, hulled and sliced
2 passionfruit

Roughly crush the meringues and divide among serving glasses.
Top with the whipped cream, strawberries and passionfruit pulp
and serve immediately. *Serves 4.*

Is it the textures and flavours or the
fact that the pavlova is now portable
that makes me fall so in love?

berry mille feuille

whipped rosewater yoghurt
with pistachio and pomegranate

You can change this tart to suit the season. Sliced stonefruit is great for summer and apple or pear for winter.

apricot tarts

I like these pears not just for dessert
but with thick yoghurt and crunchy
granola for a perfect breakfast.

vanilla pears

raspberry trifle

6 sponge finger biscuits*
2 tablespoons raspberry or orange liqueur or sherry
1½ cups fresh or frozen raspberries
1½ tablespoons icing (confectioner's) sugar
½ cup (125g) mascarpone*
½ cup (125ml) single (pouring) cream*
1 tablespoon icing (confectioner's) sugar, extra
1 teaspoon vanilla extract

Divide the sponge finger biscuits between serving glasses and sprinkle with the liqueur. Roughly mix together the raspberries and icing sugar with a fork breaking some of the raspberries and spoon over the biscuits. Place the mascarpone, cream, extra icing sugar and vanilla in a bowl and whisk until thick. Spoon mascarpone mixture over the raspberries and chill until ready to serve. *Serves 2.*

berry mille feuille

8 square wonton wrappers*
50g butter, melted
2 tablespoons icing (confectioner's) sugar
½ cup (125ml) single (pouring) cream*, whipped
125g blueberries
125g raspberries
extra icing (confectioner's) sugar, for dusting

Preheat oven to 180°C (350°F). Place the wontons on a baking tray lined with non-stick baking paper. Brush the wontons with butter and sprinkle with icing sugar. Bake for 5–7 minutes or until golden. Cool on trays. Place a wonton on each of 4 serving plates. Spoon half the cream onto the wontons and top with the blueberries. Top with another wonton and the remaining cream and sprinkle with raspberries. Dust with extra icing sugar to serve. *Serves 4.*

Store the crisp sugary wonton layers in an airtight container for up to two weeks for a perfect dessert standby.

whipped rosewater yoghurt with pistachio and pomegranate

1½ cups (420g) thick natural yoghurt
1 cup (250ml) single (pouring) cream*
1 teaspoon rosewater*
3 tablespoons honey
¼ cup (35g) roasted and shelled unsalted pistachios, roughly chopped
⅓ cup pomegranate seeds*

Place the yoghurt, cream and rosewater in a bowl and whisk until thick. Divide half the honey among serving glasses, spoon over the yoghurt mixture and top with the remaining honey, pistachios and pomegranate seeds. Serve immediately. *Serves 4.*

apricot tarts

1 x 200g sheet store-bought shortcrust pastry*, thawed
2 tablespoons apricot jam
2 tablespoons almond meal* (ground almonds)
4 apricots, halved
sugar, for sprinkling

Preheat oven to 180°C (350°F). Cut pastry into 2 x 10cm x 14cm rectangles. Place pastry on a baking tray lined with non-stick baking paper. Spread the pastry with the jam and sprinkle with the almond meal. Top with the apricots and sprinkle with sugar. Bake for 15–18 minutes or until pastry is golden. Serve with thick cream or ice-cream. *Serves 2.*

vanilla pears

2 cups (500ml) water
1 cup (220g) caster (superfine) sugar
1 vanilla bean, split and seeds scraped
4 firm brown pears, peeled, halved and cored
vanilla ice-cream or thick (double) cream*, to serve

Place the water, sugar and vanilla bean and seeds in a deep frying pan over medium-high heat and bring to the boil. Allow to simmer for 3 minutes. Add the pears and cook for 3 minutes each side or until just tender. Serve warm with some of the poaching syrup and vanilla ice-cream or thick cream. *Serves 4.*

seared figs with maple mascarpone

cheat's chocolate éclairs

deconstructed tiramisu

cheat's chocolate éclairs

1 cup (250ml) double (heavy) cream*
1 teaspoon vanilla extract
1 tablespoon icing (confectioner's) sugar, sifted
12 sponge finger biscuits*, halved lengthways
125g dark chocolate*, melted
¼ teaspoon vegetable oil

Place the cream, vanilla and sugar in a bowl and whisk gently until thick. Place the bases of the biscuits onto a wire rack. Spoon on the cream mixture and top with the remaining biscuits. Mix together the chocolate and oil. Spread chocolate mixture over the tops of the biscuits. *Makes 12.*

The cream makes the biscuits go soft after an hour or two. A good reason not to wait too long for dessert!

Use different flavoured ice-cream to tailor-make your sundae or add liqueur for a grown-up version.

cookies and cream sundae

caramelised figs with maple mascarpone

6 figs, halved
½ cup (90g) brown sugar
250g mascarpone*
⅓ cup (80ml) maple syrup

Heat a non-stick frying pan over high heat. Press the cut side of the figs into the sugar. Place the sugared side down into the pan and cook for 10–15 seconds or until the sugar is melted. Remove from pan and place on serving plates. Place a spoonful of mascarpone on each serving plate and make an indent in it with the back of the spoon. Fill each mascarpone indent with maple syrup and serve. *Serves 4.*

deconstructed tiramisu

2 tablespoons espresso coffee
1 tablespoon caster (superfine) sugar
2 tablespoons coffee liqueur
¼ cup (60g) mascarpone*
¼ cup (60ml) singe (pouring) cream*
2 teaspoons icing (confectioner's) sugar, sifted
½ teaspoon vanilla extract
6 small sponge finger biscuits*

Place the espresso and sugar in a saucepan over low heat and stir until the sugar dissolves. Simmer very slowly for 1 minute. Remove from heat, add the liqueur and chill. Place the mascarpone, cream, icing sugar and vanilla in a bowl and whisk until soft peaks form. To serve, divide the coffee mixture between 2 small serving glasses. Spoon the mascarpone mixture into 2 separate small serving glasses. Place the glasses on serving plates and serve with the biscuits. *Serves 2.*

This is my ultimate do-ahead, so easy and yet terribly chic dessert. I like to call it my dipping tiramisu.

cookies and cream sundae

2 store-bought chocolate fudge cookies, roughly crumbled
2 scoops vanilla ice-cream
⅓ cup (80ml) single (pouring) cream*, whipped
chocolate sauce
60g dark chocolate*, chopped
¼ cup (60ml) single (pouring) cream*

To make the chocolate sauce, place the chocolate and cream in a saucepan over low heat and stir until smooth. Set aside to cool. To serve, divide the crumbled cookie between serving glasses and top with the ice-cream. Top with a spoonful of whipped cream and the chocolate sauce. *Serves 2.*

cheat's chocolate hazelnut mousse

300ml single (pouring) cream*
1 tablespoon hazelnut liqueur
¼ cup (85g) chocolate hazelnut spread

Place the cream in a bowl and whisk until just starting to thicken. Stir the liqueur through the chocolate nut spread. Add to the cream and whisk gently until combined and thick. Spoon the mousse mixture into glasses and serve. *Serves 4.*

For a silky light texture, be sure not to overwhip the cream.

cheat's chocolate hazelnut mousse

mango and banana yoghurt gelato

You could easily turn this into a summer pudding by replacing the rhubarb with berries.

rhubarb pudding

mango and banana yoghurt gelato

2 bananas, peeled and chopped
3 mangoes, peeled and chopped
1 cup (280g) thick natural or vanilla yoghurt

Place the banana and mango in a sealed container and freeze
for 2–3 hours or until frozen. Place the frozen fruit and yoghurt
in a blender or food processor and blend until smooth. Serve
immediately or place in a sealed container and freeze. After
freezing allow to soften for 5 minutes before serving. *Serves 4–6.*

*This no-guilt gelato attracts kids big
and small. The banana is the secret
to the smooth and creamy texture.*

rhubarb puddings

⅔ cup (150g) caster (superfine) sugar
3 eggs
1 cup (250ml) single (pouring) cream*
1 tablespoon plain (all-purpose) flour
1 cup (120g) almond meal* (ground almonds)
1 teaspoon vanilla extract
5–6 thin stalks rhubarb
2 tablespoons granulated sugar, extra
vanilla ice-cream, to serve

Preheat oven to 180°C (350°F). Place sugar, eggs, cream, flour,
almond meal and vanilla into a bowl and whisk to combine. Spoon
mixture into 4 x 1-cup capacity (250ml) ovenproof dishes. Cut the
rhubarb into lengths to fit the tops of the puddings. Top the puddings
with the rhubarb and sprinkle with sugar. Bake for 25 minutes or until
pudding is set. Serve warm or cold with ice-cream. *Serves 4.*

coconut macaron ice-cream sandwiches

2 eggwhites
½ cup (110g) caster (superfine) sugar
2 cups (160g) desiccated coconut*
ice-cream, to serve

Preheat oven to 160°C (325°F). Place the eggwhite, sugar
and coconut in a bowl and mix to combine. Line baking trays
with non-stick baking paper. Place an egg ring on the tray and
fill with 2 tablespoons of the mixture. Press with the back of a
spoon to flatten and remove egg ring. Repeat with the remaining
mixture. Bake the macarons for 10–12 minutes or until a light
golden colour. Cool on trays. To serve, sandwich the macarons
together with your choice of ice-cream. *Serves 6.*

*The combination of the chewy macaron
with the soft ice-cream is pure magic,
so don't overcook the macaron.*

coconut macaron ice-cream sandwiches

fresh

Everything deserves a little makeover now and then. Here I take classic recipes and show you how to deliver all the flavour without the fuss. From the new Caesar salad to my chic and easy version of steak and three veg, I've worked out how to give old favourites a fresh edge without the time-consuming preparation. Who says you can't improve the classics?

fresh
savoury

Why wrestle with pastry when you can have a crispy bacon shell instead?

the new caesar salad

egg and bacon pies

the new caesar salad

8 rashers bacon, rind removed
¼ cup (60ml) maple syrup
2 baby cos (romaine) lettuces, trimmed and halved
8 long thin slices baguette, toasted
4 eggs, soft boiled and peeled
¼ cup (20g) finely grated parmesan
caesar dressing
1 egg
2 anchovy fillets
½ teaspoon Worcestershire sauce*
1 teaspoon lemon juice
¾ cup (180ml) vegetable or grape seed oil

Preheat oven to 160°C (325°F). Brush the bacon with maple syrup, place on a baking tray lined with non-stick baking paper and bake for 15 minutes or until golden. To make the dressing, place the egg, anchovy, sauce and lemon juice in a food processor and process until combined. With the motor running, gradually add the oil and process until creamy. Add water to adjust the thickness. To serve, place ingredients on plates. Top with dressing and parmesan. *Serves 4.*

egg and bacon pies

6 rashers thinly sliced bacon, rind removed
6 eggs
1 cup (240g) crème fraîche* or sour cream
2 tablespoons flat-leaf parsley leaves

Preheat oven to 180°C (350°F). Grease 4 x 12cm round pie tins and line each with 1½ rashers of bacon. In a medium bowl, whisk together the eggs, crème fraîche and parsley. Pour the egg mixture into the tins and bake for 25 minutes or until the bacon is crisp and the egg filling is just set. Serve with hot buttered toast. *Serves 4.*

How do you improve on a classic burger? Crispy pancetta might just do the trick.

gourmet beef burger

caprese salad

gourmet beef burger

500g beef mince (ground beef)
1 clove garlic, crushed
1 tablespoon tomato paste
1 tablespoon Worcestershire sauce*
2 tablespoons chopped flat-leaf parsley leaves
sea salt and cracked black pepper
8 slices pancetta*
4 burger buns, halved and toasted
4 thick slices vintage cheddar cheese
salad leaves, caramelised onion relish* or tomato chutney, to serve

Place the mince, garlic, tomato paste, sauce, parsley, salt and pepper in a bowl and mix until well combined. Shape into 4 large flat patties. Place a round of pancetta on each side of each patty. Heat a non-stick frying pan over medium-high heat. Cook the patties for 4 minutes each side or until cooked to your liking. Place the patties on the base of the toasted buns and top with cheese, salad leaves and onion or chutney. Top with remaining bun halves and serve. *Serves 4.*

caprese salad

2 large heirloom or vine-ripened tomatoes
2 x 100g buffalo mozzarella*
½ cup (80g) black olives
2 sprigs basil
1½ tablespoons olive oil
2 teaspoons balsamic vinegar
sea salt and cracked black pepper
crusty bread, to serve

Place a saucepan of water over high heat and bring to the boil. Place the tomatoes in the water for 30 seconds, remove and place in a bowl of iced water until cool. Peel away the tomato skins. Arrange tomatoes, mozzarella, olives and basil on serving plates. Drizzle with olive oil, balsamic, salt and pepper. Serve with crusty bread. *Serves 2.*

Just add some generous slices of crusty bread to make this salad the most simple but satisfying meal.

steak and three veg

1 x 300g beef eye fillet steak
sea salt and cracked black pepper
aïoli*, to serve
three veg
1 large potato, peeled and sliced with a vegetable peeler
1 sweet potato (kumara), peeled and sliced with a vegetable peeler
1 parsnip, peeled and sliced with a vegetable peeler
50g butter, melted
½ cup (40g) finely grated parmesan
1 tablespoon thyme leaves
sea salt and cracked black pepper

Preheat oven to 200°C (400°F). To make the three veg, place the potato, sweet potato and parsnip in separate bowls. Divide the butter, parmesan, thyme, salt and pepper among the bowls and toss to combine. Line a baking tray with non-stick baking paper. Pile each vegetable into 2 flat piles. Bake for 20–25 minutes or until golden and crisp. While the vegetables are cooking, cook the beef. Sprinkle the beef generously with salt and pepper. Heat a frying pan over high heat. Cook the beef for 3 minutes each side or until well browned. Place on a baking tray and bake for 4 minutes for rare and 7–8 minutes for medium. To serve, slice the beef in half and place on serving plates with the three veg. Serve with aïoli. *Serves 2.*

The dinner I grew up with was long overdue for a glamorous makeover. The result is amazing.

steak and three veg

Using whole leaves of sage gives the skewers plenty of flavour.

sage chicken skewers with spring slaw

pasta with mint pesto

french pot-roasted chicken

pasta with mint pesto

200g spaghetti
2 cups mint leaves
1 cup flat-leaf parsley leaves
⅓ cup (25g) finely grated parmesan
¼ cup (40g) blanched almonds
1 clove garlic, peeled
½ cup (125ml) light olive oil
extra finely grated parmesan and cracked black pepper, to serve

Cook the pasta in a large saucepan of boiling salted water for 8–10 minutes or until al dente. Drain and keep warm. While the spaghetti is cooking, make the mint pesto. Place the mint, parsley, parmesan, almonds and garlic in the bowl of a food processor. Slowly add the oil while the motor is running. Process until roughly chopped and combined. Spoon the pesto over the spaghetti and toss to combine. Serve with extra grated parmesan and pepper. *Serves 2.*

The perfect balance of textures and flavours is sure to make this your new favourite salad.

chicken waldorf salad

sage chicken skewers with spring slaw

4 x 125g chicken thigh fillets, trimmed
20 large sage leaves
olive oil, for brushing
2 cloves garlic, crushed
spring slaw
6 spears green asparagus, sliced with a vegetable peeler
6 spears white asparagus, sliced with a vegetable peeler
100g snow peas (mange tout), trimmed
¼ cup small chervil sprigs
¼ cup (60ml) lemon juice
1 tablespoon Dijon mustard
1 tablespoon olive oil
sea salt and cracked black pepper

To make the spring slaw, blanch the asparagus in boiling water for 3 seconds and refresh in iced water. Blanch the snow peas in boiling water for 30 seconds and refresh in iced water. Place the asparagus, snow peas and chervil in a bowl and toss to combine. Combine the lemon juice, mustard, oil, salt and pepper and pour over the slaw. To make the skewers, cut the chicken into large chunks. Thread onto skewers with the sage leaves. Combine the oil and garlic and brush over the skewers. Heat a barbecue or char-grill pan over medium-high heat. Cook the chicken skewers for 4–5 minutes each side or until cooked through. Serve with the slaw. *Serves 2.*

french pot-roasted chicken

10g dried porcini mushrooms*
⅓ cup (80ml) boiling water
8 eschalots (French shallots), peeled
2 rashers bacon, rind removed and chopped
8 small Swiss brown mushrooms
2 teaspoons olive oil
2 x 650g small chickens
1 tablespoon tarragon leaves
1 cup (250ml) chicken stock

Place the porcini in a bowl, cover with the water and set aside for 5 minutes. Heat a large saucepan over medium-high heat. Add the eschalots, bacon and Swiss browns and cook for 4 minutes or until golden. Remove from pan and set aside. Add the oil and chickens and cook for 2 minutes each side or until golden. Remove the porcini from the water and chop, reserving the porcini liquid. Return the eschalots, bacon and Swiss browns to the pan with the tarragon, porcini, porcini liquid and stock. Bring to the boil and cover with a tight-fitting lid. Reduce heat and simmer for 25 minutes or until the chicken is cooked through and tender. Serve the chickens with creamy mashed potatoes. *Serves 2.*

chicken waldorf salad

1 green apple, cored and very thinly sliced
1 bulb fennel, very thinly sliced
1 stalk of celery, sliced with a vegetable peeler
1 cup (160g) shredded cooked chicken
sea salt and cracked black pepper
walnut dressing
40g butter
⅓ cup (35g) walnuts
2 tablespoons sugar
2 tablespoons white wine vinegar

Combine the apple, fennel, celery, chicken, salt and pepper on a serving plate. To make the dressing, melt the butter in a frying pan over medium-high heat. Add the walnuts, sugar and vinegar and simmer until slightly thickened. Spoon the warm dressing over the salad to serve. *Serves 2.*

garlic prawn pasta

200g angel hair pasta or spaghetti
45g butter
1 tablespoon olive oil
4 cloves garlic, sliced
1 teaspoon dried chilli flakes
1 tablespoon shredded lemon zest
12 green (raw) prawns (shrimp), peeled, cleaned
    and halved lengthways
1 tablespoon lemon juice
¼ cup flat-leaf parsley leaves, roughly torn
sea salt and cracked black pepper

Cook the pasta in a large saucepan of boiling salted water for 8–10 minutes or until al dente. Drain and keep warm. While the pasta is cooking, heat a frying pan over medium-high heat. Add the butter and oil and cook until the butter has melted. Add the garlic, chilli and zest and cook for 2 minutes. Add the prawns and cook, stirring, for 3 minutes or until the prawns are tender. Add the pasta, juice, parsley, salt and pepper to the pan and toss to combine. Serve with a simple green salad. *Serves 2.*

Fragrant with garlic, chilli and tangy lemon, this dish is full of flavour.

garlic prawn pasta

Lemon, thyme and garlic make
classic partners for chicken.

lemon and garlic roasted chicken

cheat's goat's cheese soufflé with roasted beetroot salad

My trick of not peeling the pumpkin
and roasting it until it caramelises
gives you the sweetest flavour of all.

roasted pumpkin soup

cheat's goat's cheese soufflé with roasted beetroot salad

150g soft goat's cheese
1½ cups (375ml) single (pouring) cream*
sea salt
2 eggs, separated
2 cups (140g) fresh white breadcrumbs
roasted beetroot salad
600g baby red and golden beetroot (beets)
6 rosemary sprigs
olive oil and sea salt, for sprinkling
2 tablespoons red wine vinegar
2 tablespoons olive oil
sea salt and cracked black pepper

Preheat oven to 200°C (400°F). To make the roasted beetroot salad, trim, wash and scrub the beetroot, reserving the smaller leaves. Discard the stems. Place the beetroot and rosemary on a baking tray and sprinkle with oil and salt. Roast for 40 minutes or until tender. Set aside. To make the soufflé, place the cheese, cream, salt and egg yolks in the bowl of an electric mixer and beat until light and fluffy. Fold through the breadcrumbs. Place the eggwhites in a clean bowl and beat until soft peaks form. Fold the whites into the cheese mixture. Spoon into 4 x 1½-cup capacity (375ml) lightly greased ramekins and bake for 20–25 minutes or until puffed and golden. To serve, halve the larger beetroot and toss with the leaves. Whisk together the vinegar, oil, salt and pepper and spoon over the salad. Serve with the soufflé. *Serves 4.*

It's no secret I like to cheat. Taking a short cut or two on a soufflé just makes perfect sense to me.

lemon and garlic roasted chicken

2 x 650g small chickens
2 lemons, cut into wedges
12 cloves garlic, skin on
12 springs thyme
olive oil, for drizzling

Preheat oven to 220°C (425°F). Place the chickens in a baking dish lined with non-stick baking paper. Place 2 lemon wedges, 3 cloves of garlic and 3 sprigs of thyme in the cavity of each chicken. Place the remaining lemon, garlic and thyme in the baking dish. Drizzle with olive oil and roast for 25–30 minutes or until chickens are cooked through. Serve with roasted vegetables or a simple salad. *Serves 2.*

roasted pumpkin soup

1 x 2kg whole butternut pumpkin
1 onion
olive oil, for drizzling
sea salt
3½ cups (875ml) chicken stock
1 cup (250ml) single (pouring) cream*
1 tablespoon honey
sour cream, to serve

Preheat oven to 220°C (425°F). Cut the pumpkin in half lengthways and scoop out the seeds. Place the pumpkin, cut-side up, and onion on a baking tray. Drizzle with a little oil and sprinkle with salt. Bake for 55–60 minutes or until the pumpkin is just soft and starting to brown. Scoop the pumpkin out of the skin into a blender. Scoop the onion flesh away from its skin and add to the blender. Add 1 cup (250ml) of the chicken stock and blend until smooth. Pour the mixture into a saucepan, add remaining stock, cream and honey. Place over medium heat until soup is heated through. Serve with sour cream. *Serves 4.*

All the crunch of the perfect schnitzel
made easy, no frying required.

grilled chicken schnitzel with fennel slaw

This summer favourite teams rare beef with big, bold flavours.

rare beef salad with thai dressing

crispy pan tacos

crispy pan tacos

200g beef rump steak
olive oil, for brushing
2 teaspoons smoked paprika*
sea salt and cracked black pepper
1 x 400g can red kidney beans, drained and rinsed
¼ red onion, finely chopped
100g cherry tomatoes, finely chopped
1 cup coriander (cilantro) leaves
2 tablespoons lime juice and extra lime wedges, to serve
6 corn tortillas
120g manchego* or tasty cheese, sliced

Heat a frying pan over high heat. Brush the steak with oil and sprinkle with paprika, salt and pepper. Add to pan and cook for 2–3 minutes each side, remove from pan and thinly slice. Combine the beans, onion, tomato, coriander, lime, steak, salt and pepper in a bowl. Heat a non-stick frying pan over medium heat. Brush a tortilla with oil and place in the pan. Place some cheese on one half of a tortilla and top with some of the steak mixture. Fold over tortilla and cook for 2 minutes each side or until crisp. Repeat with remaining ingredients and serve with lime wedges. *Serves 2.*

pork and fennel meatballs

The classic flavours of fennel and apple go down a treat with crispy crackling and fall-apart meat.

cider-roasted pork belly with fennel

grilled chicken schnitzel with fennel slaw

3 slices (100g) white bread
50g butter
2 teaspoons thyme leaves
sea salt and cracked black pepper
2 x 200g chicken breast fillets, trimmed and sliced lengthways
lemon wedges, to serve
fennel slaw
1 bulb fennel, very finely sliced
2 tablespoons finely chopped chives
¼ cup flat-leaf parsley leaves
2 tablespoons store-bought whole-egg mayonnaise*
1 tablespoon lemon juice
1 tablespoon water

Place the bread, butter, thyme, salt and pepper in the bowl of a food processor and process in short bursts until mixture makes fine crumbs. Place the chicken on a baking tray and top generously with the crumb mixture. Place under a preheated hot grill and grill for 7–8 minutes or until chicken is cooked through and crumbs are golden. To make the fennel slaw, combine the fennel, chives and parsley. Whisk together the mayonnaise, lemon juice and water and toss through the fennel mixture. Serve the salad with the schnitzel and lemon wedges. *Serves 2.*

rare beef salad with thai dressing

250g beef eye fillet
olive oil, for brushing
sea salt and cracked black pepper
2 Lebanese cucumbers, sliced with a vegetable peeler
½ red onion, sliced
1 long red chilli*, thinly sliced
1 cup basil leaves
thai dressing
1 tablespoon fish sauce*
2 tablespoons lime juice
4 finely shredded kaffir lime leaves*
1 tablespoon caster (superfine) sugar

Heat a frying pan over high heat. Brush the beef with a little oil and sprinkle generously with salt and pepper. Cook the beef for 2–3 minutes on all sides or until well browned. Set aside to rest. To make the dressing, combine the fish sauce, lime juice, lime leaves and sugar. To serve, thinly slice the beef and divide between serving plates with the cucumber, onion, chilli and basil. Spoon over the dressing to serve. *Serves 2.*

pork and fennel meatballs

2½ teaspoons fennel seeds
2 teaspoons sea salt flakes
1 cup (70g) fresh breadcrumbs
¼ cup (60ml) milk
750g pork mince (ground pork)
100g piece flat pancetta*, finely chopped
¼ cup chopped flat-leaf parsley
olive oil, for cooking
crusty bread, olive tapenade, sliced tomato and rocket (arugula)
    leaves, to serve

Preheat oven to 180°C (350°F). Place the fennel seeds and salt in a mortar and pestle and lightly crush. Place the breadcrumbs and milk in a bowl and stand for 5 minutes. Add the mince, pancetta, parsley and fennel-salt mixture and mix well for 2–3 minutes or until mixture comes together. Shape ⅓ cupfuls of the mixture into balls. Heat a non-stick frying pan over medium-high heat. Add a little oil to the pan and cook the meatballs, in batches, until well browned on all sides. Place on a baking tray and bake for 5–7 minutes or until cooked through. Serve the meatballs with crusty bread, olive tapenade, sliced tomato and rocket leaves. *Serves 4.*

cider-roasted pork belly with fennel

1kg pork belly
sea salt
8 sprigs lemon thyme
4 bulbs fennel, halved
1½ cups (375ml) cider

Preheat oven to 220°C (425°F) or the hottest your oven will go. Dry the pork well using absorbent paper. Score the skin at even intervals using a sharp knife. Place the pork in a baking dish and generously rub salt into the skin. Tuck the lemon thyme under the pork and roast for 45 minutes or until the skin has crackled and is crisp. Reduce the heat to 120°C (250°F). Add the fennel to the pan and carefully add enough cider to almost cover the meat but not touch the skin of the pork. Bake for 1 hour, turning the fennel once, or until the pork is tender and the cider has reduced. To serve, slice the pork into pieces and serve with the fennel and pan juices. *Serves 4.*

potato and blue cheese frittata

Greek salad gets a makeover with a piece of pan-fried feta. I love the molten, crispy crust.

grilled feta greek salad

potato and blue cheese frittata

12 small red or chat (baby) potatoes, cooked and sliced
2 teaspoons chopped rosemary leaves
sea salt and cracked black pepper
6 eggs
1½ cups (375ml) single (pouring) cream*
100g blue cheese, coarsely chopped
buttered toast, to serve

Preheat oven to 160°C (325°F). Place the potato, rosemary, salt and
pepper in a 2-litre (8-cup) capacity ovenproof dish. Whisk together
the eggs and cream. Pour over the potato mixture and sprinkle with
the blue cheese. Bake for 25–30 minutes or until the eggs are just
set. Serve on thick slices of hot buttered toast. *Serves 4.*

grilled feta greek salad

2 Lebanese cucumbers, sliced lengthways
4 small vine-ripened tomatoes, halved
1 cup (150g) pitted mixed olives
½ red onion, thinly sliced
¾ cup mint leaves
¾ cup flat-leaf parsley leaves
200g firm feta, thickly sliced
olive oil, for brushing
honey dressing
2 tablespoons red wine vinegar
2 tablespoons olive oil
1 tablespoon honey
sea salt and cracked black pepper

To make the dressing, whisk together the vinegar, oil, honey, salt and
pepper. Divide the cucumber, tomato, olives, onion, mint and parsley
between serving plates. Brush the feta with oil. Heat a non-stick
frying pan over high heat. Cook the feta for 2 minutes each side or
until golden. Place on top of the salad. Spoon the dressing over the
salad to serve. *Serves 2.*

lamb roasted with rosemary, feta and garlic

1 small boned leg lamb (1.6kg), trimmed
sea salt and cracked black pepper
2 heads garlic, cloves separated and skin on
8 sprigs rosemary
1 tablespoon olive oil
350g firm feta, thickly sliced
2 stalks celery, sliced with a vegetable peeler
100g baby or wild rocket (arugula)
1 tablespoon lemon juice
1 tablespoon olive oil, extra
lemon wedges, to serve

Preheat oven to 180°C (350°F). Heat a large frying pan over high
heat. Sprinkle both sides of the lamb generously with salt and pepper.
Add to the pan and cook for 4 minutes each side or until well browned.
Place the lamb in a baking dish lined with non-stick baking paper and
toss with the garlic, rosemary and oil. Add the feta to the pan and bake
for 25 minutes for medium or until cooked to your liking. To serve,
slice the lamb and serve with the roasted feta and the garlic squeezed
from its skin. Toss together the celery, rocket, lemon juice and extra
oil and serve with the lamb and lemon wedges. *Serves 4.*

I love a recipe that's big on flavour but short on time. Rosemary, garlic and salty feta are just perfect.

lamb roasted with rosemary, feta and garlic

eggs on toast

speedy roasted chicken and chips

chicken pies

speedy roasted chicken and chips

1.6kg chicken
2 teaspoons smoked paprika*
2 teaspoons thyme leaves
1 teaspoon sea salt flakes
½ teaspoon cracked black pepper
2 tablespoons vegetable oil
4–5 large potatoes, scrubbed and cut into fat chips
lemon wedges, to serve

Preheat oven to 200°C (400°F). Using kitchen scissors, cut down either side of the backbone of the chicken and discard the bone. Flatten the chicken and place in a baking dish skin-side up. Combine the paprika, thyme, salt, pepper and oil. Brush some of the mixture over the chicken. Place the potatoes in a baking tray lined with non-stick baking paper. Toss with the remaining paprika mixture. Bake the potatoes for 10 minutes then add the chicken to the tray and bake for 30 minutes or until the chicken is cooked through and the chips are crisp. Serve with the lemon wedges. *Serves 4.*

The perfect fast pea soup gets even better with a fresh hit of mint and the salty bite of crispy prosciutto.

pea and ham soup

eggs on toast

4 large slices sourdough bread
butter, for spreading
4 eggs
15g butter, extra
½ teaspoon grated lemon rind
150g baby spinach leaves
sea salt and cracked black pepper
shaved parmesan, to serve
truffle oil, if desired

Heat a large frying pan over low heat. Make a hole in the middle of each piece of bread. Butter both sides of the bread. Place bread in the frying pan and cook covered for 3–4 minutes or until golden. Turn the bread and crack an egg into each hole of the bread. Cook for 2 minutes or until eggs are cooked to your liking. Place on serving plates. Add extra butter and lemon rind to the pan and cook for 1 minute. Add the spinach, salt and pepper and stir until wilted. Serve with the eggs, top with shaved parmesan and drizzle with truffle oil, if desired. *Serves 2.*

I'm sure no one will complain when served this version of eggs on toast.

chicken pies

2 cups (320g) coarsely chopped cooked chicken
¾ cup (180g) sour cream
2 tablespoons chopped basil leaves
1 teaspoon finely grated lemon rind
2 teaspoons Dijon mustard
sea salt and cracked black pepper
4 x 200g sheets store-bought butter puff pastry*, thawed
1 egg, lightly beaten

Preheat oven to 180°C (350°F). Combine the chicken, sour cream, basil, lemon rind, mustard, salt and pepper. Cut 2 x 15cm x 10cm rectangles from the pastry and place on a baking tray lined with non-stick baking paper. Spoon the filling into the centre of the pastry. Brush just inside the edge of the pastry with the egg. Cut 2 x 18cm x 12cm rectangles from the remaining pastry and place over the filling. Gently press the edges together to seal. Brush the tops of the pies with the beaten egg. Bake the pies for 25–30 minutes or until pastry is puffed and golden. *Serves 2.*

pea and ham soup

2 teaspoons olive oil
1 onion, finely chopped
1½ cups (180g) frozen peas
1 potato, peeled and grated
1 litre (4 cups) chicken stock
¼ cup mint leaves
½ cup (125ml) single (pouring) cream*
sea salt and cracked black pepper
6 slices prosciutto*

Heat a saucepan over medium heat. Add the oil and onion and cook for 4 minutes or until soft. Add the peas, potato and stock and bring to the boil. Cook for 6 minutes or until peas are tender. Add the mint, cream, salt and pepper. Place the pea mixture in a blender and blend until almost smooth. Return the soup to the pan. Preheat a grill on high heat. Grill the prosciutto for 1 minute or until just crisp. Break the prosciutto into pieces and stir through the soup. *Serves 2.*

pork loin with stilton and port and honey glaze

1kg pork loin rack
salt
12 sprigs oregano
2 large sweet potatoes (kumara), peeled and quartered
150g stilton*, thickly sliced
port and honey glaze
1 cup (250ml) port
¼ cup (60ml) beef stock
2 tablespoons honey

Preheat oven to 220°C (425°). Score the skin of the pork at 1cm intervals using a sharp knife. Rub the skin with salt and place in a baking dish on top of the oregano. Roast for 20 minutes, then reduce the heat to 180°C (350°F). Add the sweet potato to the pan and cook for a further 30 minutes or until pork is cooked to your liking. While the pork is roasting, make the port and honey glaze. Place the port, stock and honey in a saucepan over medium heat. Allow mixture to simmer for 12–15 minutes or until glaze is reduced and syrupy. To serve, slice the pork and place on serving plates with the sweet potato. Top the pork with the stilton and spoon over the port and honey glaze. *Serves 4.*

There are some recipes that leave a lasting impression. This is one of them.

pork loin with stilton, port and honey glaze

chicken sung choi bao

I love the fact that wonton wrappers are the perfect size and thickness for simple home-made ravioli.

pumpkin ricotta ravioli

Nothing speaks more of summer than these roasted vegetables with basil dressing. Just add sunshine.

roasted summer ratatouille

chicken sung choi bao

1 tablespoon red curry paste*
1 tablespoon olive oil
2 x 200g chicken breast fillets, trimmed
1 Lebanese cucumber, sliced with a vegetable peeler
150g snow peas (mange tout), shredded and blanched
⅓ cup coriander (cilantro) leaves
⅓ cup mint leaves
4–6 iceberg lettuce cups
¼ cup (60ml) coconut cream*
1 tablespoon lime juice
sea salt

Preheat grill on high heat. Combine the curry paste and oil and spread over the top of the chicken. Place on a baking tray and cook under a hot grill for 7–8 minutes or until cooked through. Set aside to cool slightly. Combine the cucumber, snow peas, coriander and mint and divide between the lettuce cups. Combine the coconut cream, juice and salt and pour over the salad in the cups. Slice the chicken and place in the lettuce cups to serve. *Serves 2.*

Layers of crunch, a spicy kick and cooling coconut cream give this hand-held meal plenty of appeal.

pumpkin ricotta ravioli

550g pumpkin, peeled and chopped
1 tablespoon olive oil
250g ricotta
½ cup (40g) finely grated parmesan
1 tablespoon oregano leaves, roughly chopped
1 tablespoon flat-leaf parsley leaves, roughly chopped
sea salt and cracked black pepper
20 wonton wrappers*
finely grated parmesan, extra, to serve
brown butter sauce
50g butter
4 sprigs oregano

Preheat oven to 220°C (425°F). Place pumpkin on a baking tray lined with non-stick baking paper. Sprinkle with oil and bake for 20–25 minutes or until golden. Combine the ricotta, parmesan, oregano, parsley, salt and pepper. Place 2 teaspoons of the ricotta mixture and 2 pieces of pumpkin on half the wontons. Brush the wonton edges with water and top with remaining wontons. Press the edges to seal. To make the brown butter sauce, cook the butter and oregano in a saucepan over low heat until butter is lightly browned and oregano is crisp. Cook the ravioli in a large saucepan of boiling salted water for 3–4 minutes or until al dente. Drain and serve with remaining pumpkin, brown butter sauce and extra parmesan. *Serves 2.*

roasted summer ratatouille

3 small vine-ripened tomatoes, halved
3 small yellow zucchini (courgette), halved
2 small long red capsicum (bell peppers), halved and seeds removed
3 baby eggplant (aubergine), halved
8 cloves garlic, skin on
2 tablespoons olive oil
sea salt and cracked black pepper
10 baby bocconcini*
char-grilled sourdough slices, to serve
basil dressing
¼ cup small basil leaves
1 tablespoon white balsamic vinegar*
1 tablespoon olive oil

Preheat oven to 220°C (425°F). Place the tomato, zucchini, capsicum, eggplant and garlic on a baking tray and drizzle with the oil, salt and pepper. Bake for 20 minutes or until soft and slightly golden. To make the basil dressing, place the basil, vinegar and oil in a blender and blend until almost smooth. To serve, place vegetables, bocconcini and bread on serving plates and spoon over the basil dressing. *Serves 2.*

veal with soft polenta

The perfect way to cook ribs is with a sticky, tasty dry spice rub.

spice-roasted ribs

ricotta shells with roasted tomato sauce

ricotta shells with roasted tomato sauce

16 large pasta shells
500g ricotta
½ cup (40g) finely grated parmesan
2 egg yolks
sea salt and cracked black pepper
10 sprigs thyme
olive oil, for drizzling
extra finely grated parmesan, to serve
roasted tomato sauce
4 cloves garlic, sliced
6 Roma tomatoes, thickly sliced

Preheat oven to 200°C (400°F). Cook the pasta shells in a large saucepan of boiling salted water for 8 minutes or until al dente. Drain. Combine the ricotta, parmesan, yolks, salt and pepper. Fill shells with ricotta mixture. To make the roasted tomato sauce, place the garlic and tomato in an ovenproof dish. Drizzle with olive oil. Roast for 20 minutes or until tomato is soft. Top with pasta shells, sprinkle with thyme and drizzle with olive oil. Cover and roast for a further 10 minutes or until heated through. Serve with extra parmesan. *Serves 2.*

cheesy quiche

The crunchy combination of winter veg dressed in lively buttermilk makes the perfect partner to pork.

thyme and orange pork with winter slaw

veal with soft polenta

4 x 90g veal steaks
sea salt and cracked black pepper
20g butter
4 slices prosciutto*
6–8 sprigs sage
lemon wedges, to serve
soft polenta
1 cup (250ml) milk
1 cup (250ml) chicken stock
½ cup (85g) instant polenta*
½ cup (40g) finely grated parmesan
sea salt and cracked black pepper
2 tablespoons mascarpone*

To make the soft polenta, place the milk and stock in a saucepan over high heat and bring to the boil. Whisk in the polenta and cook, stirring, until smooth. Stir through the parmesan, salt and pepper, cover and set the polenta aside. Heat a large frying pan over high heat. Sprinkle the veal with salt and pepper. Place the butter, veal, prosciutto and sage in the pan and cook for 2 minutes each side or until the veal is cooked to your liking and the prosciutto is crisp. To serve, divide the polenta between serving plates and top with a spoonful of mascarpone. Add the veal, prosciutto and sage to the plates and serve with a wedge of lemon. *Serves 2.*

Soft polenta has all the same qualities as mashed potato, only it's faster.

spice-roasted ribs

1kg American-style pork spare ribs or baby back ribs
2 teaspoons smoked paprika*
1 teaspoon chilli powder
¼ cup (55g) brown sugar
2 teaspoons salt

Preheat oven to 160°C (325°F). Cut the ribs into 4 sections. Combine the paprika, chilli, sugar and salt. Rub generously over both sides of the ribs and place on a baking tray lined with non-stick baking paper. Cover with aluminium foil and roast for 1 hour. Remove the cover and increase heat to 220°C (425°F). Bake for 15–20 minutes or until browned. Serve with a simple salad and thick-cut chips. *Serves 2.*

cheesy quiche

6 sheets filo pastry*
40g butter, melted
4 eggs
1½ cups (375ml) single (pouring) cream*
½ cup (125ml) milk
⅓ cup (25g) finely grated parmesan
1 teaspoon chopped tarragon leaves, optional

Preheat oven to 160°C (325°F). Brush each sheet of pastry with butter and layer on top of each other. Trim the edges of the pastry and then cut the pastry into 4 pieces and press into 4 x 1-cup capacity (250ml) lightly greased muffin tins. To make the filling, place the eggs, cream, milk and parmesan in a bowl and whisk to combine. Pour the egg mixture into the pastry shells, sprinkle with tarragon and bake for 20–25 minutes or until just set. Serve with a green salad. *Serves 4.*

thyme and orange pork with winter slaw

2 teaspoons olive oil
1 tablespoon shredded orange zest
1 teaspoon thyme leaves
4 x 80g pork loin steaks
sea salt and cracked black pepper
¼ cup (60ml) orange juice
1 tablespoon brown sugar
winter slaw
1 small celeriac (celery root), peeled and finely sliced
1 fennel, finely sliced
1 cup finely shredded cabbage
¼ cup flat-leaf parsley leaves
¼ cup (60ml) buttermilk
1 tablespoon lemon juice
sea salt and cracked black pepper

To make the winter slaw, place the celeriac, fennel, cabbage and parsley in a bowl and toss to combine. Combine the buttermilk, juice, salt and pepper and pour over the slaw. Toss to combine and set aside. Heat a frying pan over high heat. Add the oil, orange zest and thyme and cook for 3 minutes or until crisp. Remove from pan and set aside. Sprinkle the pork with salt and pepper and add to the pan. Cook for 3 minutes each side or until well browned. Remove from the pan and set aside. Add the orange juice and sugar to the pan and cook until reduced. Return the pork and orange zest mixture to the pan and cook pork for 1 minute each side or until heated through. Serve with the winter slaw and pan juices. *Serves 2.*

Leftover rice never looked so good.
Just add prawns, chilli and a
paper-thin omelette.

prawn fried rice

thai-inspired fish and chips

prawn fried rice

2 eggs, lightly beaten
2 teaspoons sesame oil*
1 tablespoon vegetable oil
2 teaspoons grated ginger
1 long red chilli*, finely sliced
4 green onions (scallions), finely sliced
10 large green (raw) prawns (shrimp), peeled and cleaned
4 cups cooked jasmine rice
soy and chilli sauces, to serve

Heat a non-stick frying pan over medium heat. Add half the sesame oil and half the egg and swirl to coat the pan. Cook for 1 minute or until the egg has set. Remove from pan, set aside and repeat with remaining egg and oil. Heat the frying pan over high heat. Add the vegetable oil, ginger, chilli and onion and cook for 1 minute. Add the prawns and cook for 3 minutes. Add the rice and cook for 2–3 minutes or until warmed through. Place the omelettes on serving plates and spoon over the rice mixture. Drizzle with soy and chilli sauces to serve. *Serves 2.*

thai-inspired fish and chips

2 x 500g small whole fish, scaled, gutted and cleaned
1 cup (200g) rice flour*
vegetable oil, for deep frying
800g sweet potato (kumara), peeled and finely sliced
coriander (cilantro) leaves and lime wedges, to serve
chilli sauce
3 long red chillies*, deseeded and sliced
¼ cup shredded ginger
2 tablespoons fish sauce*
⅓ cup (80ml) lime juice
⅓ cup (75g) caster (superfine) sugar

To make the chilli sauce, place the chilli, ginger, fish sauce, juice and sugar in a frying pan over medium-high heat and bring to the boil. Reduce heat and allow to simmer for 5 minutes or until syrupy. To cook the fish, score the flesh of the fish and sprinkle with rice flour, shaking off any excess. Heat oil in a wok over high heat until very hot. Cook the fish, one at a time, for 2–3 minutes each side or until golden and crisp. Drain on absorbent paper and keep warm. Cook the sweet potato, in batches, until crisp, then drain. To serve, place the fish and sweet potato chips onto serving plates. Serve with the chilli sauce, coriander leaves and lime wedges. *Serves 2.*

I make double the chilli sauce and use it as a dipping sauce for rice paper rolls and steamed dumplings.

lime and lemongrass chicken

6 large slices ginger
6 kaffir lime leaves*
4 stalks lemongrass, white part only, trimmed
1 long red chilli*, trimmed
1 tablespoon vegetable oil
4 x 125g chicken thigh fillets, halved
1½ cups (375ml) coconut milk*
1 tablespoon fish sauce*
80g baby spinach leaves
coriander (cilantro) leaves, to serve

Place the ginger, lime leaves, lemongrass and chilli in the bowl of a small food processor and process until finely chopped. Heat a frying pan over medium-high heat. Add the oil and the lime leaf mixture and cook, stirring, for 4 minutes or until fragrant. Add the chicken and cook for 1 minute each side. Add the coconut milk and fish sauce and simmer the chicken for 7 minutes each side or until chicken is tender. Stir through the spinach and serve with steamed rice and coriander leaves. *Serves 2.*

Making spice paste from scratch sometimes seems a chore, until I remember the flavour of this dish.

lime and lemongrass chicken

The perfect carbonara should be a creamy, cheesy delight.

pasta carbonara

salt and pepper prawns

spinach and feta pies

salt and pepper prawns

750g green (raw) king prawns (shrimp)
2 tablespoons sea salt flakes
2 teaspoons chilli powder
2 teaspoons Chinese five-spice*
2 teaspoons cracked black pepper
1 cup (200g) rice flour*
vegetable oil, for deep frying
lemon wedges, to serve

Cut the prawns along the back of the shell using kitchen scissors and devein. Rinse and pat dry. Place the salt, chilli, five-spice and pepper in a bowl and mix well. Combine half the spice mix with the flour, toss the prawns in the rice flour mixture and shake off any excess. Heat oil in a deep frying pan or wok over high heat until hot. Cook the prawns, in batches, for 2–3 minutes or until crisp and cooked through. Drain on absorbent paper and while still hot, sprinkle with some of the remaining spice mixture. Serve with lemon wedges. *Serves 2.*
+ If you want to eat the whole prawn, use smaller school prawns.

spring minestrone

pasta carbonara

200g fettuccine or thick pasta
2 egg yolks
1 cup (250ml) single (pouring) cream*
⅓ cup (25g) finely grated parmesan cheese
sea salt and cracked black pepper
4–6 slices prosciutto*
extra finely grated parmesan, to serve

Cook the pasta in a large saucepan of boiling salted water for 8–10 minutes or until al dente. Drain, return to the pan and place over low heat. Add the egg yolks, cream, parmesan, salt and pepper and stir for 2 minutes or until the sauce has thickened slightly and coated the pasta. Place on serving plates and top with torn pieces of prosciutto. Sprinkle with extra parmesan to serve. *Serves 2.*

spinach and feta pies

6 sheets filo pastry*
40g butter, melted
250g frozen spinach, thawed
500g ricotta
2 eggs
⅓ cup (25g) finely grated parmesan cheese
¼ cup finely chopped mint leaves
sea salt and cracked black pepper
75g feta, roughly chopped

Preheat oven to 180°C (350°F). Brush each filo sheet with butter and place one on top of the other. Cut the stack of pastry sheets in half so you have 2 rectangles and place on baking trays lined with non-stick baking paper. Squeeze the excess liquid from the spinach and place in a bowl with the ricotta, eggs, parmesan, mint, salt and pepper and mix to combine. Divide the filling between the two pastries leaving a 5cm border. Fold over the pastry edges to form a border. Sprinkle the filling with feta. Bake for 35 minutes or until pastry is golden and filling has set. *Serves 2.*

No wonder this pie has become one of my favourites. The filling and fold-over pastry is simplicity itself.

spring minestrone

1 litre (4 cups) chicken stock
1 cup (160g) fresh peas
4 yellow squash, thinly sliced
100g sugar snap peas, trimmed
8 stalks asparagus, sliced
100g green beans, trimmed and chopped
1 teaspoon finely grated lemon rind
4 long slices baguette
100g goat's cheese
1 teaspoon lemon thyme leaves
¼ cup small chervil sprigs
sea salt and cracked black pepper

Place the chicken stock in a saucepan over medium-high heat and bring to the boil. Add the peas, squash, snap peas, asparagus, beans and lemon rind and cook for 5 minutes or until the vegetables are tender. Spread the baguette with combined goat's cheese and thyme. Place under a preheated hot grill and cook until golden. To serve, ladle the soup into bowls and sprinkle with chervil, salt and pepper. Serve with the cheese toasts. *Serves 2.*

niçoise salad with roasted garlic vinaigrette

8 chat (baby) potatoes, halved
olive oil, for brushing
sea salt and cracked black pepper
8 cloves garlic, skin on
2 x 175g tuna steaks
2 tablespoons salted capers, rinsed
¼ cup (60ml) olive oil
1 tablespoon white wine vinegar
100g green beans, trimmed and blanched
⅓ cup (60g) small black olives

Preheat oven to 180°C (350°F). Toss the potato in a little oil and salt and place on a baking tray with the garlic. Bake for 20–25 minutes or until the potatoes are golden and garlic is soft. Brush the tuna with a little olive oil and sprinkle with pepper. Heat a frying pan over high heat. Add the tuna and capers and cook for 2 minutes each side or until the tuna is well seared. To make the dressing, squeeze the garlic from its skin and whisk together with the oil and vinegar. To assemble, place the potato, beans, olives and capers on serving plates. Top with the tuna and spoon over the dressing. *Serves 2.*

I love all the robust flavours in this salad, from salty olives to peppery tuna and aromatic garlic.

niçoise salad with roasted garlic vinaigrette

fresh
sweet

Any fruit that doesn't lose its shape when cooked is perfect for this galette.

peach crumble galette

no-fuss banana caramel pudding

no-fuss banana caramel pudding

175g butter, softened and chopped
1 cup (175g) brown sugar
½ cup (110g) caster (superfine) sugar
½ teaspoon ground cinnamon
1 cup mashed banana
3 eggs
2 cups (300g) self-raising (self-rising) flour
½ teaspoon baking powder
caramel sauce
1½ cups (375ml) single (pouring) cream*
¾ cup (135g) brown sugar

Preheat oven to 170°C (325°F). To make the pudding, place the butter, sugars, cinnamon, banana, eggs, flour and baking powder in the bowl of an electric mixer and beat on medium speed for 1 minute or until just combined. Pour the mixture into a greased 28cm x 8cm loaf tin lined with non-stick baking paper and bake for 1 hour or until cooked when tested with a skewer. To make the caramel sauce, place the cream and brown sugar in a saucepan and simmer for 10 minutes or until thickened. Slice the pudding and pour over the warm sauce. *Serves 8.*

caramelised apple pies

baked whole lemon pudding

You can't go past the tropical, fresh flavours of coconut, sweet mango and tangy lime. Delicious.

coconut jelly with mango

The subtle tang of the buttermilk
gives this version of panna cotta
a lovely lightness and freshness.

buttermilk panna cotta

peach crumble galette

350g store-bought or home-made sweet shortcrust pastry*
3 tablespoons apricot jam
3 peaches, sliced
vanilla ice-cream, to serve
crumble topping
40g butter, softened
2 tablespoons slivered almonds, finely chopped
¼ cup (35g) plain (all-purpose) flour
2 tablespoons caster (superfine) sugar
½ teaspoon ground cinnamon

Preheat oven to 200°C (400°F). Roll out pastry between 2 sheets
of non-stick baking paper into a rough round about 5mm thick. Place
the pastry on a baking tray lined with non-stick baking paper. Spread
the pastry with the jam leaving a 5cm border. Top the jam with the
peaches. Fold over the pastry to form a rim. To make the crumble
topping, combine the butter, almonds, flour, sugar and cinnamon.
Sprinkle in clumps over the top of the peaches. Bake for 25 minutes
or until pastry and the crumble top are golden. Serve warm with
vanilla ice-cream. *Serves 4.*

caramelised apple pies

4 x 200g sheets store-bought puff pastry, thawed
4 small apples, cored and thinly sliced
90g butter, melted
½ cup (90g) brown sugar
1 teaspoon ground cinnamon
vanilla ice-cream, to serve

Preheat oven to 180°C (350°F). Cut 4 x 15cm pastry rounds to fit
4 x 12cm round pie dishes. Place the apple in a bowl and toss with the
butter, sugar and cinnamon. Arrange apples on top of the pastry and
bake for 30 minutes or until the apples are soft and caramelised. Serve
warm with vanilla ice-cream or cream. *Serves 4.*

*Life's too short to make your own
puff pastry; store-bought is just fine.*

baked whole lemon pudding

1 thin-skinned lemon
1½ cups (330g) caster (superfine) sugar
30g butter, melted
3 egg yolks
¾ cup (180ml) single (pouring) cream*
2 tablespoons cornflour (cornstarch)
vanilla ice-cream, to serve

Preheat oven to 160°C (325°F). Cut the lemon into 8 pieces and
remove any seeds. Place in a food processor with the sugar and process
until very smooth. Add the butter, egg yolks, cream and cornflour
and process until smooth. Pour mixture into 4 greased 1-cup capacity
(250ml) ovenproof pie dishes. Bake for 22–24 minutes or until just
set. Serve warm or cold with vanilla ice-cream. *Serves 4.*

coconut jelly with mango

2 teaspoons warm water
1 teaspoon powdered gelatine*
2 cups (500ml) coconut cream*
¼ cup (55g) caster (superfine) sugar
2 teaspoons lime juice
½ teaspoon vanilla extract
fresh mango and lime wedges, to serve

Place the water in a small bowl and sprinkle over the gelatine. Set aside
until the gelatine has absorbed the water. Place the coconut cream,
sugar, lime juice and vanilla in a saucepan over medium heat and bring
to the boil. Add the gelatine mixture and stir for 1 minute. Remove
from heat and pour into 4 greased ½-cup capacity (125ml) moulds
or ramekins. Refrigerate for 4 hours or until jellies are firm. Turn the
jellies out and serve with mango and a squeeze of lime. *Serves 4.*

buttermilk panna cotta

2 tablespoons warm water
1½ teaspoons powdered gelatine*
1 cup (250ml) single (pouring) cream*
½ cup (110g) caster (superfine) sugar
2 teaspoons vanilla extract
2 cups (500ml) buttermilk
fresh passionfruit pulp, to serve

Place the water in a small bowl and sprinkle over the gelatine. Set aside
until the gelatine has absorbed the water. Place the cream and sugar
in a saucepan over medium heat and stir to dissolve the sugar. Add the
gelatine and stir to dissolve. Remove from heat and stir through the
vanilla and buttermilk. Pour mixture into 4 glasses and refrigerate for
3 hours or until set. Serve with passionfruit. *Serves 4.*

standby brownies

This is my new low-fuss version of the classic jam and cream tart.

jam tarts

chocolate cherry cakes

chocolate cherry cakes

125g dark chocolate*, chopped
155g butter
3 eggs
⅓ cup (75g) caster (superfine) sugar
⅔ cup (100g) plain (all-purpose) flour
¼ teaspoon baking powder
1 cup (120g) almond meal* (ground almonds)
¼ cup (60ml) brandy
12 cherries
whipped single (pouring) cream*, to serve

Preheat oven to 160°C (325°F). Place the chocolate and butter in a small saucepan over low heat and stir until smooth. Place eggs, sugar, flour, baking powder, almond meal, brandy and chocolate mixture in a bowl and mix to combine. Spoon mixture into greased shallow cupcake tins and press a cherry into the top. Bake for 12–15 minutes or until the cake is just set. Serve with whipped cream. *Makes 12.*

This lighter version combines all the things you love about crème brûleé but without all the work.

cheat's raspberry brulée

standby brownies

150g butter
1¼ cups (275g) caster (superfine) sugar
¾ cup (75g) cocoa
1 teaspoon vanilla extract
3 eggs
½ cup (75g) plain (all-purpose) flour

Preheat oven to 160°C (325°F). Place the butter, sugar and cocoa in a saucepan over low heat and stir until the butter has melted. Spoon into a bowl and add the vanilla and eggs, whisking well. Sift the flour over the mixture and whisk to combine. Spoon the mixture into a 20cm-square cake tin lined with non-stick baking paper. Bake for 30–35 minutes or until centre is just set. Cool in tin and cut into squares to serve. *Makes 16.*

In our household, even the cooking chocolate disappears. Hence why these rich brownies are made with cocoa.

jam tarts

12 round gow gee wrappers*
50g butter, melted
⅓ cup (75g) caster (superfine) sugar
½ cup (160g) strawberry jam
½ cup (125ml) single (pouring) cream*, whipped
raspberries or strawberries, to serve

Preheat oven to 180°C (350°F). Brush the wrappers with butter and sprinkle lightly with sugar. Place in shallow patty tins, buttered-side up, and bake for 6 minutes or until golden. Cool in tin. Fill the tart shells with jam and whipped cream and top with raspberries or a slice of strawberry to serve. *Makes 12.*

cheat's raspberry brulée

300g frozen raspberries
⅓ cup (75g) caster (superfine) sugar
1½ cups (420g) Greek-style thick natural yoghurt
1 cup (250ml) double (heavy) cream*
2 tablespoons caster (superfine) sugar, extra
1 teaspoon vanilla extract
extra caster (superfine) sugar, for sprinkling

Place raspberries and sugar in a saucepan over high heat and simmer for 20 minutes or until the raspberry mixture thickens. Spoon the raspberry mixture into 4 x 1-cup capacity (250ml) ovenproof dishes. Refrigerate until cold. Whisk together the yoghurt, cream, sugar and vanilla until thick and spoon over the raspberry mixture. Refrigerate until cold. Sprinkle with sugar and caramelise the sugar with a kitchen blow torch until golden. *Serves 4.*

cheat's chocolate fondant

¼ cup (50g) plain (all-purpose) flour, sifted
½ cup (55g) icing (confectioner's) sugar, sifted
¾ cup (90g) almond meal* (ground almonds)
2 eggwhites
100g butter, melted
160g dark chocolate*, melted
4 small squares dark chocolate, extra

Preheat oven to 150°C (300°F). Place the flour, sugar, almond meal, eggwhites, butter and melted chocolate in a bowl and mix well to combine. Spoon half the mixture into 4 x ½-cup capacity (125ml) lightly greased dariole moulds. Divide the extra chocolate squares between the moulds and top with the remaining mixture. Bake for 20–25 minutes or until cooked but soft in the middle. Stand in tins for 5–7 minutes before turning out. *Serves 4.*

Take the guesswork out of making the perfect fondant and cheat a little for a stellar result.

cheat's chocolate fondant

pistachio baklava cigars with rosewater syrup

These muffins are so easy to make, I could bake them in my sleep.

too-easy blueberry muffins

pistachio baklava cigars with rosewater syrup

4 sheets filo pastry*
60g butter, melted
¾ cup (105g) shelled unsalted roasted pistachios, chopped
⅓ cup (75g) caster (superfine) sugar
1 teaspoon ground cinnamon
extra chopped pistachios, to serve
rosewater syrup
¼ cup (60ml) water
½ cup (110g) sugar
½ teaspoon rosewater*

Preheat oven to 200°C (400°F). Brush a sheet of filo pastry with butter. Combine the pistachios, sugar and cinnamon. Sprinkle one half of the length of the filo with a quarter of the mixture. Fold over the filo to enclose the nut mixture, cut in half and roll each half into a cigar shape. Repeat with remaining filo and nut mixture. Place on a baking tray and bake for 15–20 minutes or until golden and crisp. While the cigars are baking, make the rosewater syrup. Place the water and sugar in a saucepan over medium heat and bring to the boil. Allow to simmer for 3 minutes, then remove from heat. Stir in the rosewater. Place the warm filo cigars onto serving plates and spoon over the syrup and extra pistachios to serve. *Serves 4.*

Using filo can be tricky. Keep the pastry covered with a damp tea towel while you are working with it.

too-easy blueberry muffins

2½ cups (375g) self-raising (self-rising) flour, sifted
1 teaspoon baking powder
1 cup (220g) caster (superfine) sugar
½ cup (125ml) vegetable oil
1 egg
½ cup (125ml) milk
1 teaspoon vanilla extract
300g fresh or frozen blueberries
granulated sugar, for sprinkling

Preheat oven to 180°C (350°F). Place the flour, baking powder and sugar in a bowl. Place the oil, egg, milk and vanilla in a separate bowl and whisk to combine. Pour the liquid ingredients into the dry ingredients and mix until just combined. Add the blueberries and mix to combine. Spoon mixture into a 12-hole ½-cup capacity (125ml) muffin tin lined with paper patty cases. Sprinkle the tops with sugar and bake for 30–35 minutes or until cooked when tested with a skewer. Remove from tin and cool on a wire rack. *Makes 12.*

baked passionfruit custards

1 cup (250ml) milk
1 cup (250ml) single (pouring) cream*
3 eggs
1 egg yolk, extra
⅓ cup (75g) caster (superfine) sugar
½ cup (125ml) passionfruit pulp (approximately 4 passionfruit)

Preheat oven to 160°C (325°F). Place the milk and cream in a saucepan over low heat and heat until hot but not boiling. Place the eggs, yolk and sugar in a bowl and whisk until pale. Slowly whisk in the hot milk mixture. Strain the mixture back into the saucepan then add the passionfruit. Return to the heat and stir over low heat for 3 minutes until the mixture has thickened slightly. Pour the mixture into 4 x ¾-cup capacity (180ml) ramekins or heatproof dishes and place in a baking dish. Fill the baking dish with enough hot water to come halfway up the sides of the ramekins. Bake for 20 minutes or until custards are just set. Remove from baking dish and refrigerate for 2–3 hours or until cold. *Serves 4.*

This dessert combines the comforting pleasure of custard with a kiss of passionfruit sunshine. Bliss.

baked passionfruit custards

simple

If there is a short cut, I'm proud to say I think I've found it. This is a selection of all the short-order tricks I've picked up over the years. I'll show you how to take fresh ingredients and a few store-bought staples and turn them into a collection of recipes that are bound to become sure-fire standbys. Cheating isn't just allowed; it's encouraged!

It's the simple cheats that are often the best. Like quince paste on lamb.

quince lamb with blue cheese polenta

moroccan couscous with spiced chicken

quince lamb with blue cheese polenta

6 x 50g lamb cutlets, trimmed
1 tablespoon quince paste*
sea salt and cracked black pepper
50g rocket (arugula) leaves
blue cheese polenta
2 cups (500ml) chicken stock
1 cup (250ml) milk
¾ cup (120g) instant polenta*
80g blue cheese, crumbled

To make the blue cheese polenta, place the stock and milk in a saucepan over high heat and bring to the boil. Add the polenta and stir for 2–3 minutes or until creamy. Spoon polenta into a small greased ceramic dish and refrigerate until set. When set, cut the polenta into two pieces. To cook the lamb and polenta, place the lamb cutlets on a tray, spread with quince paste and sprinkle with salt and pepper. Add the polenta slices to the tray and top with the blue cheese. Preheat a grill on high heat. Place lamb and polenta under the grill and cook for 3–4 minutes or until lamb is cooked to your liking. Place on serving plates with the rocket and serve. *Serves 2.*

moroccan couscous with spiced chicken

1 cup (200g) couscous*
1½ cups (375ml) hot chicken stock
20g butter
½ cup mint leaves
½ cup flat-leaf parsley leaves
¼ cup pomegranate seeds*
1 teaspoon finely grated orange rind
sea salt and cracked black pepper
2 x 200g chicken breast fillets, trimmed and sliced
olive oil, for brushing
1 tablespoon za'atar*
120g marinated feta*

Place the couscous in a bowl and pour over the boiling stock. Cover with plastic wrap and set aside until the stock has absorbed. Stir through the butter. Stir through the mint, parsley, pomegranate, orange rind, salt and pepper. To cook the chicken, heat a frying pan over medium heat. Brush the chicken with oil and sprinkle with za'atar. Cook for 3 minutes each side or until chicken is cooked through. Place couscous on serving plates and top with chicken and feta to serve. *Serves 2.*

summer tomato pasta

For me, creamy white beans make an excellent cheat's substitute for mash.

seared beef with garlic white beans

summer tomato pasta

200g spaghetti
300g cherry tomatoes
2 zucchini (courgette), sliced with a vegetable peeler
1 tablespoon lemon juice
1 tablespoon olive oil
1 clove garlic, crushed
⅓ cup basil leaves
⅓ cup mint leaves
sea salt and cracked black pepper
1 buffalo mozzarella*, torn into pieces

Cook the pasta in a large saucepan of boiling salted water for 8–10 minutes or until al dente. Drain. While the pasta is cooking, make an incision in each tomato using a small, sharp knife. Tear in half, squeeze out the seeds and discard. Toss the pasta with the tomato, zucchini, lemon juice, olive oil, garlic, basil, mint, salt and pepper. Divide the pasta between serving plates and top with mozzarella to serve. *Serves 2.*

Sometimes the sweetest and softest ripe summer tomatoes are just too good to cook.

seared beef with garlic white beans

4 x 125g thinly cut new york or small rump steaks
sea salt and cracked black pepper
50g rocket (arugula) leaves
garlic white beans
2 tablespoons olive oil
1 teaspoon rosemary leaves
6 cloves garlic, sliced
1 x 400g can white (cannellini) beans, rinsed and drained
1 teaspoon grated horseradish
1 tablespoon lemon juice

To make the garlic white beans, heat a frying pan over medium heat. Add the oil, rosemary and garlic and cook for 1 minute. Add the beans, horseradish, lemon juice, salt and pepper and cook for 3 minutes or until heated through. Set aside and keep warm. Heat the frying pan over high heat. Sprinkle steaks with salt and pepper and cook for 2 minutes each side or until cooked to your liking. To serve, layer the beans, steaks and rocket on serving plates. *Serves 2.*

roasted tomato and mozzarella salad

2 ox heart or heirloom tomatoes, halved
4–8 large basil leaves
2 x 125g buffalo mozzarella*, halved
4 slices char-grilled sourdough bread
2 tablespoons olive tapenade
4 slices prosciutto*
40g rocket (arugula) leaves
olive oil, for drizzling

Preheat grill on high heat. Line a baking tray with non-stick baking paper. Scoop out the seeds and some of the soft flesh from the tomatoes and discard. Place the tomatoes on the baking tray cut-side up. Line the tomatoes with basil leaves and top with mozzarella. Grill for 3–4 minutes or until the mozzarella is golden. To serve, spread char-grilled bread with tapenade and top with prosciutto and rocket. Place the tomato on the plates and drizzle with olive oil to serve. *Serves 2.*

This recipe knows no time. It's just as perfect for brunch, lunch or dinner.

roasted tomato and mozzarella salad

one-pot chinese chicken

I don't usually consider pasta delicate, however this spring version is just that.

pasta with asparagus and taleggio

simple thai fish cakes

pasta with asparagus and taleggio

200g fettucine or pappardelle
12 asparagus spears, sliced with a vegetable peeler
2 tablespoons olive oil
1 tablespoon lemon juice
¼ cup small basil leaves
sea salt and cracked black pepper
100g taleggio*, thickly sliced

Cook the pasta in a large saucepan of salted boiling water for 8–9 minutes or until almost al dente. Add the asparagus and cook for 30 seconds or until tender. Drain and return to the warm pan. Add the oil, lemon juice, basil, salt and pepper and toss to combine. Divide the pasta mixture between serving bowls and top with the taleggio. *Serves 2.*

roasted sourdough and bacon salad

one-pot chinese chicken

3 cups (750ml) chicken stock
6 slices ginger
4 cloves garlic, halved
1 long green chilli*, sliced
1½ cups (300g) jasmine rice
4 x 125g chicken thigh fillets, halved
4 green onions (scallions), sliced
1 cup coriander (cilantro) leaves
soy sauce, to serve

Place the stock, ginger, garlic and chilli in a deep frying pan over high heat and bring to the boil. Add the rice and stir once to distribute evenly over the bottom of the pan. When the stock comes back to the boil, add the chicken. Cover, reduce heat to low and cook for 20 minutes or until the rice has absorbed the stock and the chicken is tender. Top the chicken and rice with the onion and coriander and serve with soy sauce. *Serves 2.*

I would cook a version of this recipe every few weeks – it just works.

simple thai fish cakes

500g firm white fish fillets, skin off
2 teaspoons finely grated ginger
2 tablespoons chilli jam*
¼ cup coriander (cilantro) leaves
1 eggwhite
vegetable oil, for shallow frying
lime wedges, to serve
cucumber and lime salad
1 tablespoon lime juice
2 teaspoons fish sauce*
1½ teaspoons caster (superfine) sugar
3 Lebanese cucumbers, sliced with a vegetable peeler
¼ cup mint leaves
¼ cup coriander (cilantro) leaves

Place the fish, ginger, chilli jam, coriander and eggwhite in the bowl of a food processor and process until smooth. With slightly wet hands shape the mixture into 12 flat cakes. Heat a non-stick frying pan over medium-high heat. Add 1cm of oil and cook the fish cakes, in batches, for 3–4 minutes each side or until cooked through. To make the cucumber and lime salad, place the lime juice, fish sauce and sugar in a bowl and mix to combine. Add the cucumber, mint and coriander and toss to coat. Serve with the fish cakes and lime wedges. *Serves 4.*

roasted sourdough and bacon salad

250g sourdough bread, torn
6 cloves garlic, peeled
4 rashers bacon, rind removed
6 small or cherry tomatoes, halved
50g curly endive (frisée) leaves
¼ cup (60g) sour cream
1 teaspoon Dijon mustard
2 teaspoons lemon juice
finely grated parmesan, to serve

Preheat oven to 180°C (350°F). Place bread, garlic and bacon on a baking tray lined with non-stick baking paper. Bake for 20 minutes or until bread and garlic are golden and bacon is crisp. Place on serving plates with the tomatoes and endive. Combine the sour cream, mustard and lemon juice. Spoon the dressing over the salad and sprinkle with parmesan to serve. *Serves 2.*

pasta with goat's curd, caramelised red onion and fig

1 tablespoon olive oil
4 red onions, thinly sliced
1 teaspoon rosemary leaves
4 soft dried figs, thinly sliced
½ cup (125ml) beef stock
⅓ cup (80ml) white wine vinegar
¼ cup (45g) brown sugar
sea salt and cracked black pepper
200g pappardelle or fettucine
100g goat's curd or soft goat's cheese
olive oil and finely grated parmesan, to serve

Place the oil, onion, rosemary, fig, stock, vinegar and sugar in a frying pan over high heat and bring to the boil. Reduce heat to a rapid simmer, cover and cook, stirring occasionally, for 8–10 minutes or until the onions are soft and caramelised. Add salt and pepper to taste. While the onions are cooking, cook the pasta in a large saucepan of boiling salted water for 8–10 minutes or until al dente. Drain, toss the onion through the pasta and divide between serving bowls. Top with goat's curd, olive oil and parmesan to serve. *Serves 2.*

If you love a pasta with lots of rich layers of flavour, this one is sure to satisfy. It's sweet and robust.

pasta with goat's curd, caramelised red onion and fig

When cooking with salmon or ocean
trout, I like to add sharp flavours
like wasabi to cut through the richness.

crispy-skin trout with watercress and radish salad

roasted potato salad with feta and mint

field mushroom galette

crispy-skin trout with watercress and radish salad

2 teaspoons wasabi paste*
sea salt
1 tablespoon olive oil
4 x 150g ocean trout fillets, skin on
3 cups watercress sprigs
10 radishes, trimmed and very thinly sliced
lemon-soy dressing
2 tablespoons lemon juice
2 tablespoons soy sauce
2 teaspoons sesame oil*
2 teaspoons finely grated ginger

To make the lemon-soy dressing, whisk together the lemon juice, soy, sesame oil and ginger. To cook the trout, mix together the wasabi, salt and olive oil and brush over the fish. Preheat a non-stick frying pan over high heat. Add the trout, skin-side down, and cook for 5–6 minutes or until the skin is golden and crisp. Turn the fish and cook for 1 minute or until cooked to your liking. Combine the watercress and radish and divide among serving plates. Add the trout and spoon over the dressing to serve. *Serves 4.*

roasted potato salad with feta and mint

6 kipfler (waxy) or fingerling potatoes, scrubbed and halved
olive oil, for drizzling
sea salt
1 cup (120g) frozen peas, blanched
200g feta*, cut into large slices
6 slices prosciutto*
½ cup mint leaves
dijon dressing
1 tablespoon olive oil
1 tablespoon white wine vinegar
1 teaspoon Dijon mustard

Preheat oven to 180°C (350°F). Place the potato on a baking tray and toss with a little olive oil and sea salt. Bake for 25 minutes or until golden and tender. Set aside to cool slightly. To make the dressing, combine the oil, vinegar and mustard. To serve, toss the potato and peas with half the dressing. Divide the feta, prosciutto, potato, peas and mint leaves between serving plates. Spoon over remaining dressing to serve. *Serves 2.*

field mushroom galette

500g store-bought or home-made shortcrust pastry*
30g butter
1 clove garlic, crushed
6–8 field mushrooms, sliced
2 teaspoons lemon thyme leaves
sea salt and cracked black pepper
1 cup (200g) ricotta
1 tablespoon shredded lemon zest
½ leek, finely sliced
2 teaspoons olive oil

Preheat oven to 200°C (400°F). Roll out the pastry on a lightly floured surface into a rough, 5mm-thick round shape and place on a baking tray lined with non-stick baking paper. Set aside. To make the mushroom filling, heat a large frying pan over high heat. Add the butter and garlic and cook for 30 seconds. Add the mushrooms and cook for 5 minutes, turning occasionally, until golden brown. Stir through the thyme, salt and pepper. Allow the mixture to cool. Spread the ricotta over the pastry leaving a 5cm border. Top with the lemon zest and the mushroom mixture. Fold the excess pastry over to create a rough border. Toss the leek with the oil and sprinkle over the filling. Bake the tart for 20 minutes or until the pastry is golden and crisp. Serve with a simple green salad. *Serves 2.*

Why struggle with pastry in a tin when a free-form folded version is just so easy, rustic and chic.

cashew and chilli beef stir-fry

So elegant and light, this dish is perfect for a special spring lunch.

salmon and soy bean noodle salad with wasabi dressing

roasted carrot and parsnip salad

roasted carrot and parsnip salad

3 carrots, peeled and quartered
3 parsnips, peeled and quartered
2 tablespoons oil
1½ teaspoons ground cumin
2 tablespoons honey
½ cup coriander (cilantro) leaves
85g labne* or creamy feta*
⅓ cup (45g) roasted hazelnuts, halved
1 teaspoon sumac*

Preheat oven to 200°C (400°F). Place the carrot and parsnip in a ceramic baking dish. Combine the oil, cumin and honey and pour half of the mixture over the vegetables. Cover and cook for 15 minutes, then uncover and cook for a further 15 minutes or until the vegetables are tender. Divide vegetables between serving plates and top with the coriander, labne and hazelnuts. Pour over remaining honey mixture as a dressing and sprinkle with sumac. *Serves 2.*

barbecued red curry chicken with snow pea salad

This is another summer favourite
of mine that came about after
I combined two recipes.

warm white bean and tuna salad

cashew and chilli beef stir fry

2 tablespoons vegetable oil
3 long red chillies*, sliced
4 cloves garlic, sliced
300g beef eye fillet, sliced
sea salt and cracked black pepper
150g green beans, trimmed
½ cup (75g) roasted unsalted cashew nuts
½ cup basil leaves
steamed jasmine rice, to serve

Heat a frying pan or wok over high heat. Add the oil, chilli, and garlic and cook for 1–2 minutes or until chilli is crisp. Remove from pan and set aside. Sprinkle the beef with salt and pepper and add to the hot pan. Cook for 1 minute or until sealed. Add the chilli mixture and beans and cook, stirring, for 3 minutes. Roughly chop half the cashews, add whole and chopped nuts to the pan and toss to combine. Place on serving plates and top with basil. Serve with steamed jasmine rice. *Serves 2.*

This dry style of stir-fry has lots of big flavours of chilli and garlic, balanced by crisp green beans.

salmon and soy bean noodle salad with wasabi dressing

150g soba noodles*
450g frozen soy beans* (edamame), shelled and blanched
1 cup mustard cress or watercress
8 thin slices sashimi salmon
8 red radishes, finely sliced
wasabi dressing
2 teaspoons wasabi paste*
2 tablespoons vegetable or peanut oil
2 tablespoons light soy sauce

Cook the noodles in a large saucepan of rapidly boiling salted water until al dente. Drain and rinse under cold water. Combine the noodles, soy beans and cress and divide between serving bowls. Top with the salmon and radish. To make the wasabi dressing, whisk together the wasabi, oil and soy and pour over the salad. *Serves 2.*

barbecued red curry chicken with snow pea salad

1 tablespoon Thai red curry paste*
1 tablespoon lime juice
1 tablespoon vegetable oil
2 x 200g chicken breast fillets, trimmed and cut lengthways
1 sweet potato (kumara), scrubbed and thinly sliced
extra vegetable oil, for brushing
snow pea salad
100g snow peas (mange tout), shredded
30g snow pea shoots or salad leaves
¼ cup (60ml) coconut cream*
1 tablespoon lime juice
1 tablespoon fish sauce*

Combine the curry paste, lime juice and oil. Brush over the chicken and set aside to marinate for 5 minutes. To make the snow pea salad, pour boiling water over the snow peas to soften, then drain and refresh under cold water. Combine with the snow pea shoots. To make the dressing, combine the coconut cream, juice and fish sauce. To cook the chicken, heat a barbecue or char-grill pan over high heat. Brush the sweet potato with oil. Cook the chicken and sweet potato for 3 minutes each side or until tender. Place on serving plates with the snow pea salad and spoon over the dressing to serve. *Serves 2.*

warm white bean and tuna salad

1 tablespoon olive oil
2 cloves garlic, crushed
pinch dried chilli flakes
1 tablespoon salted capers, rinsed
1 x 400g can white (cannellini) beans, drained and rinsed
½ cup flat-leaf parsley leaves
2 x 150g tuna fillets
extra olive oil, for brushing
sea salt and cracked black pepper
1 tablespoon sumac*
lemon wedges, to serve

Heat a frying pan over medium-high heat. Add the oil, garlic, chilli and capers and cook for 3 minutes. Add the beans and cook for 4 minutes or until heated through. Remove from heat and set aside. To cook the tuna, brush both sides with the extra oil and sprinkle well with salt and pepper. Heat a frying pan over high heat. Cook the tuna for 1–2 minutes each side or until cooked to your liking. Remove from pan and thickly slice. To serve, stir the parsley though the bean mixture and divide between serving plates. Top with the sliced tuna, sprinkle with sumac and serve with lemon wedges. *Serves 2.*

miso-roasted chicken

The secret to this dish is the chilli jam. It's loaded with garlic, ginger and shrimp paste for a real flavour kick.

chilli pork with snake beans

miso-roasted chicken

⅓ cup (75g) white miso paste*
2 teaspoons sesame oil*
⅓ cup (80ml) mirin*
2 x 200g chicken breast fillets, trimmed
3 baby eggplant (aubergines), halved
olive oil, for brushing
1 tablespoon sesame seeds
noodles and wilted baby spinach leaves, to serve

Preheat a grill on high heat. Place the miso, sesame oil and mirin in a bowl and mix to combine. Place the chicken and eggplant, cut-side up, into a baking dish lined with non-stick baking paper and brush the eggplant with a little oil. Spoon the miso mixture over the chicken and eggplant and sprinkle with sesame seeds. Place under the hot grill and cook for 18–20 minutes, until chicken is cooked through and eggplant is tender. Serve with noodles and wilted baby spinach leaves. *Serves 2.*

The miso lends the chicken a lovely sweet and elegant nutty flavour.

chilli pork with snake beans

¼ cup (80g) chilli jam*
350g pork mince (ground pork)
1 x 200g can water chestnuts*, drained and sliced
1 tablespoon lime juice
½ cup coriander (cilantro) leaves
½ cup basil leaves
400g snake beans
lime wedges, to serve

Heat a non-stick frying pan over high heat. Add the chilli jam and pork and cook stirring for 5–7 minutes or until the pork is cooked through. Stir through the chestnuts, lime juice, coriander and basil. Steam the snake beans until tender and place on serving plates. Spoon over the chilli pork and serve with lime wedges. *Serves 2.*

hoisin and ginger pork dumpling soup

350g pork mince (ground pork)
1 tablespoon finely grated ginger
2 tablespoons hoisin sauce*
1 tablespoon rice flour*
1 green onion (scallion) finely chopped
1 litre (4 cups) chicken stock
½ cup (125ml) Shaoxing* (Chinese rice wine) or dry sherry
¼ teaspoon Chinese five-spice*
250g fresh shanghai or udon noodles*, rinsed
3 baby bok choy*, leaves separated
finely sliced long red chilli*, to serve

Place the pork, ginger, hoisin, flour and spring onion in a bowl and mix to combine. Shape tablespoonfuls of the mixture into round dumplings and set aside. Place the stock, Shaoxing and five-spice in a large saucepan over high heat. Add the dumplings and cook for 5 minutes or until cooked through, remove with a slotted spoon and set aside. Add the noodles to the stock and simmer for 2 minutes or until almost tender. Add the bok choy and cook for 1 minute. Return the dumplings to the pan and cook for 1–2 minutes or until heated through. Divide the dumplings and noodle soup between bowls and sprinkle with chilli. *Serves 2.*

It's all the flavour of your favourite Chinese dumplings only faster. Silky noodles, well-flavoured broth and crunchy greens complete the picture.

hoisin and ginger pork dumpling soup

I use this fresh coriander dressing on so many other dishes. It's such a vibrant pick-me-up.

ginger-poached chicken with coriander dressing

prawn, lemon and leek risotto

caramelised onion, gorgonzola and pumpkin galette

prawn, lemon and leek risotto

1 tablespoon olive oil
30g butter
1 leek, finely sliced
1 tablespoon shredded lemon zest
1 cup (200g) arborio rice*
2½ cups (625ml) chicken stock
12 green (raw) prawns (shrimp), peeled, cleaned with tails intact
1 tablespoon lemon juice
¼ cup flat-leaf parsley leaves
sea salt and cracked black pepper

Preheat oven to 200°C (400°F). Heat an ovenproof saucepan over medium-high heat. Add the oil, butter, leek and zest and cook for 6 minutes or until the leek is golden brown. Add the rice and stock. Cover with a tight-fitting lid and bake in the oven for 25 minutes. Add the prawns and cook for a further 5 minutes. Stir though the lemon juice, parsley, salt and pepper and serve immediately. *Serves 2.*

fried squid with preserved lemon

ginger-poached chicken with coriander dressing

1½ cups (375ml) chicken stock
12 slices ginger
2 x 200g chicken breast fillets, trimmed
175g bunch broccolini*, trimmed
coriander dressing
⅓ cup (90g) tahini*
2 tablespoons water
2 tablespoons lemon juice
2 teaspoons white wine vinegar
1 clove garlic, crushed
½ cup coriander (cilantro) leaves
¼ cup flat-leaf parsley leaves
sea salt and cracked black pepper

To make the coriander dressing, place the tahini, water, lemon juice, vinegar, garlic, coriander, parsley, salt and pepper in a blender and blend until smooth. Place stock, ginger and chicken in a large saucepan over medium heat. Bring to the boil, then reduce heat to simmer. Simmer for 6 minutes then add the broccolini and cook for a further 3 minutes or until chicken is cooked through and broccolini is tender. Remove chicken from pan and slice. Place on serving plates with the broccolini and spoon over the coriander dressing. *Serves 2.*

caramelised onion, gorgonzola and pumpkin galette

500g store-bought or home-made shortcrust pastry*
450g pumpkin, peeled and chopped
¾ cup (240g) store-bought caramelised onion relish*
150g gorgonzola*, chopped
sea salt and cracked black pepper
16 sage leaves

Preheat oven to 200°C (400°F). Steam the pumpkin until almost tender. Set aside to cool. Divide pastry in half and roll each piece between 2 sheets of non-stick baking paper to a rough, 5mm-thick round shape. Line 2 baking trays with non-stick baking paper and place a pastry round on each. Top each pastry with the caramelised onion, leaving a 5cm border. Sprinkle with gorgonzola. Place the pumpkin onto the galettes, sprinkle with salt and pepper and top with sage. Fold in the pastry to make a rough border. Bake for 25 minutes or until pastry is golden and crisp and the pumpkin is soft. *Serves 2.*

fried squid with preserved lemon

8 baby squid tubes, cleaned and halved
2 tablespoons olive oil
1½ tablespoons shredded preserved lemon rind*
2 cloves garlic, crushed
1 long red chilli*, thinly sliced
1 tablespoon salted capers, rinsed
¼ cup dill leaves
lemon wedges, store-bought whole-egg mayonnaise* and thick-cut chips, to serve

Place the squid, oil, preserved lemon, garlic, chilli and capers in a bowl and allow to marinate for 15 minutes. Heat a frying pan over high heat. Add the squid and cook, in small batches, for 1–2 minutes or until squid is tender. Divide squid mixture between serving plates. Sprinkle with dill and serve with lemon wedges, mayonnaise and thick-cut chips. *Serves 2.*

mussels with tomato and garlic baguette

1 tablespoon olive oil
2 cloves garlic, crushed
⅓ cup (50g) chopped sun-dried tomatoes
½ teaspoon dried chilli flakes
1kg mussels, scrubbed
¼ cup (60ml) dry white wine
¼ cup finely shredded basil leaves
sea salt and cracked black pepper
garlic baguette
45g butter, softened
2 cloves garlic, crushed
1 small baguette, halved

Heat a saucepan over medium-high heat. Add the oil, garlic, tomato and chilli and cook for 1 minute. Add the mussels and white wine, cover and cook for 6–8 minutes or until the mussels have opened. Discard any unopened mussels. To make the garlic baguette, mix together the butter and garlic and spread over the cut sides of the baguette. Place under a preheated hot grill and cook until golden. Stir the basil, salt and pepper through the mussels and serve with the garlic baguette. *Serves 2.*

Mopping up the tasty pan juices
with crunchy baguette is allowed.
In fact, it would be rude not to!

mussels with tomato and garlic baguette

My love of cabbage only started when I tasted it roasted. It's something about the crisp brown edges and soft leaves.

roasted pork and cabbage

roasted chicken and chorizo

smoky chilli chicken burger

roasted pork and cabbage

4 x 200g pork loin chops
2 thick slices Savoy cabbage
40g butter, melted
2 tablespoon oregano leaves
2 tablespoons honey
sea salt and cracked black pepper

Preheat oven to 200°C (400°F). Place pork and cabbage in a baking dish lined with non-stick baking paper. Drizzle the pork and cabbage with butter and sprinkle with oregano, honey, salt and pepper. Bake for 15–20 minutes or until pork and cabbage are golden and tender. Serve with pan juices. *Serves 2.*

roasted chicken and chorizo

1.6kg chicken, cut into pieces
2 chorizo*, halved lengthways
¾ cup (90g) large green olives
250g truss cherry tomatoes
8 sprigs oregano, halved
1 lemon, cut into wedges
12 cloves garlic, skin on
1 tablespoon olive oil
sea salt and cracked black pepper

Preheat oven to 200°C (400°F). Line a baking tray with non-stick baking paper. Add the chicken, chorizo, olives, tomatoes, oregano, lemon, garlic, oil, salt and pepper and toss to combine. Bake for 30–35 minutes or until chicken is cooked through and the chorizo is crisp. Discard the lemon wedges before serving. *Serves 4.*

smoky chilli chicken burger

1 tablespoon olive oil
1 teaspoon smoked sweet paprika*
1 teaspoon dried chilli flakes
2 x 200g chicken breast fillets, trimmed and sliced lengthways
2 bread rolls, halved
rocket (arugula) leaves, to serve
lemon mayonnaise
¼ cup (85g) store-bought whole-egg mayonnaise*
1 tablespoon lemon juice

To make the lemon mayonnaise, place the mayonnaise and lemon juice in a bowl and mix to combine. Combine the oil, paprika and chilli and pour over the chicken. Preheat a barbecue or char-grill pan over high heat. Cook the chicken for 2 minutes each side or until cooked through. Spread the rolls with the lemon mayonnaise and top with the rocket and chicken to serve. *Serves 2.*

I don't like to over-complicate a burger but that doesn't mean this version isn't packed with flavour.

Peas and mint have always been great allies. Add crispy chorizo, leek and pasta and it's close to perfect.

torn pasta with chorizo and peas

roasted cauliflower and hazelnut salad

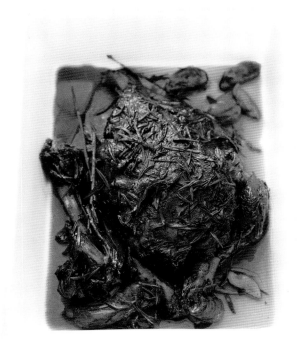

slow-cooked balsamic and garlic lamb

roasted cauliflower and hazelnut salad

500g cauliflower, cut into florets
2 tablespoons olive oil
1 red onion, cut into 8 pieces
½ cup (70g) hazelnuts, skins removed and halved
2 thin slices crusty bread, toasted
100g soft blue cheese
1¼ cups maché (lamb's lettuce)
sea salt and cracked black pepper
crème fraîche dressing
¼ cup (60g) crème fraîche*
1 tablespoon lemon juice
2 teaspoons Dijon mustard

Preheat oven to 220°C (425°F). Line a baking dish with non-stick baking paper. Add the cauliflower, oil and onion and bake for 25 minutes. Add the hazelnuts and bake for a further 5 minutes or until the cauliflower and nuts are golden. To make the dressing, whisk together the crème fraîche, lemon juice and mustard. Spread toast with blue cheese and place on serving plates. Top with cauliflower mixture, maché, salt and pepper. Spoon over the dressing. *Serves 2*.

simple beef pie

Once you master this tart, the variations are endless. You can add different toppings to taste.

tomato goat's cheese tart

torn pasta with chorizo and peas

4 sheets fresh store-bought pasta sheets, torn
1 tablespoon olive oil
3 chorizo*, sliced
1 leek, finely sliced
1 cup (120g) frozen peas, blanched
1 tablespoon lemon juice
½ cup mint leaves
finely grated parmesan, to serve

Cook the pasta in a large saucepan of boiling salted water for 8–10 minutesor until al dente. Drain. While the pasta is cooking, heat a frying pan over high heat. Add the oil, chorizo and leek and cook for 5–6 minutes, turning occasionally, until chorizo and leek are golden. Toss the chorizo mixture, peas, lemon juice and mint through the pasta. Divide between serving plates and top with a generous amount of parmesan. *Serves 2.*

slow-cooked balsamic and garlic lamb

1kg lamb shoulder, on the bone
1⅓ cups (310ml) balsamic vinegar
3 cups (750ml) chicken stock
6 sprigs rosemary
8 cloves garlic
2 tablespoons brown sugar

Preheat oven to 140°C (275°F). Place the lamb, vinegar, stock, rosemary, garlic and sugar in a deep baking dish and cover with a tight-fitting lid. Bake for 3 hours. Turn the lamb and bake for a further 2 hours. Remove the lid, increase temperature to 180°C (350°F) and bake for 30 minutes or until the lamb has browned. Remove lamb from the pan and keep warm. Pour the pan juices over a large bowl of ice and quickly remove the ice and the solidified fat with a slotted spoon. Place the pan juices into a small saucepan and bring to the boil. Serve the lamb with crispy roasted potatoes, steamed greens and the pan juices. *Serves 4.*

This recipe is my Sunday favourite. I pop it in the oven just after lunch to ensure a perfect stress-free and delicious Sunday night feast.

simple beef pie

4 x 200g sheets store-bought puff pastry*, thawed
2 x 200g beef eye fillet or sirloin steaks
sea salt and cracked black pepper
¼ cup (80g) store-bought tomato relish or caramelised onion relish*
1 egg, lightly beaten
tomato sauce (ketchup), to serve

Preheat oven to 200°C (400°F). Cut the pastry into 2 x 15cm rounds for the bases and 2 x 17cm rounds for the tops. Heat a frying pan over high heat. Sprinkle the steaks with salt and pepper and cook for 1 minute each side or until browned and sealed. Set aside to cool slightly. Place the pastry bases onto baking trays. Top with the steak and the relish. Top with the pastry tops, press edges to seal and brush with egg. Bake for 15–20 minutes or until pastry is puffed and golden. Serve with extra relish or tomato sauce (ketchup). *Serves 2.*

These pies are for the short-cut cook who expects big results.

tomato goat's cheese tart

2 x 200g sheets store-bought shortcrust pastry*, thawed
150g goat's cheese, sliced
150g red and yellow cherry tomatoes, halved
olive oil, for sprinkling
sea salt and cracked black pepper
rocket topping
50g wild rocket (arugula) leaves
2 tablespoons shredded basil leaves
1 tablespoon store-bought balsamic glaze*
shaved parmesan cheese, to serve

Preheat oven to 180°C (350°F). Cut the pastry into 2 x 18cm circles and place on a baking tray lined with non-stick baking paper. Top each pastry with the goat's cheese and tomato. Sprinkle with oil, salt and pepper and bake for 25 minutes or until pastry is golden. To make the topping, combine the rocket and basil. Pile on top of the tarts, drizzle with balsamic glaze and add parmesan to serve. *Serves 2.*

This is my favourite weeknight vegetable soup because there's next to no chopping involved.

easy vegetable soup

caramelised onion, potato and feta tart

easy vegetable soup

2 teaspoons olive oil
1 onion, finely chopped
2 cloves garlic, crushed
2 teaspoons lemon thyme leaves
2 cups (500ml) tomato purée (tomato sauce)
2 cups (500ml) chicken stock
1 carrot, peeled and grated
1 zucchini (courgette), peeled and grated
1 parsnip, peeled and grated
sea salt and cracked black pepper
finely grated parmesan, to serve

Heat a saucepan over medium-high heat. Add the oil, onion, garlic and thyme and cook for 3 minutes or until soft. Add the tomato, stock, carrot, zucchini and parsnip. Cover and bring to the boil. Allow to simmer rapidly for 15 minutes or until the vegetables are tender. To serve, ladle into bowls and top with salt, pepper and parmesan. *Serves 2.*

caramelised onion, potato and feta tart

375g store-bought frozen puff pastry*, thawed
¾ cup (240g) store-bought caramelised onion relish* or chutney
2 chat (baby) potatoes, cooked and thickly sliced
100g feta*
4 slices pancetta*
2 teaspoons rosemary leaves
sea salt and cracked black pepper
simple rocket (arugula) salad, to serve

Preheat oven to 180°C (350°F). Roll out the pastry on a lightly floured surface until 5mm thick. Roughly cut 2 x 15cm x 18cm rectangles from the pastry and place on baking trays lined with non-stick baking paper. Top the pastry with the caramelised onion leaving a 2cm border around the edge. Arrange the potato, feta and pancetta over the onion and sprinkle with rosemary, salt and pepper. Bake for 25 minutes or until the tarts are puffed and golden. Serve with a simple rocket salad. *Serves 2.*

baked pumpkin and sage risotto

1 tablespoon olive oil
1 onion, chopped
12 sage leaves
2 cups (400g) arborio rice*
800g pumpkin, peeled and chopped into small pieces
1.25 litres (5 cups) chicken stock
sea salt and cracked black pepper
30g butter
½ cup (40g) finely grated parmesan
extra finely grated parmesan and fried sage leaves, to serve

Preheat oven to 200°C (400°F). Heat a large ovenproof saucepan over medium-high heat. Add the oil and onion and cook for 3 minutes or until soft. Add the sage and cook for 1 minute. Add the rice, pumpkin and stock and cover with a tight-fitting lid. Bake for 30 minutes. The risotto will be quite liquid. Stir through the salt, pepper, butter and parmesan and stir for 2 minutes until the risotto thickens slightly. Sprinkle with extra parmesan and fried sage leaves to serve. *Serves 4.*

Why stir risotto for half an hour when you can just as easily bake it in the oven for the same result?

baked pumpkin and sage risotto

simple
sweet

Such little effort for such delicious chocolatey sweet rewards.

chocolate and cinnamon wontons

chocolate-raspberry bread pudding

chocolate-raspberry bread pudding

250g coarsely chopped dark chocolate*
1½ cups (375g) single (pouring) cream*
3 eggs
½ cup (110g) caster (superfine) sugar
1 teaspoon vanilla extract
125g sourdough bread, crusts removed and cubed
1 cup fresh or frozen raspberries

Preheat oven to 160°C (325°F). Place the chocolate and cream in a saucepan over low heat and stir until melted. Remove from heat. Place chocolate mixture, eggs, sugar and vanilla in a bowl and whisk to combine. Fold through the bread and raspberries. Spoon the mixture into 4 x 1½-cup capacity (375ml) ramekins or tea cups and place in a baking dish. Fill with enough boiling water to come halfway up the sides of the ramekins. Bake for 30–35 minutes until the pudding is puffed and just set. *Serves 4.*

ultimate one-bowl chocolate dessert cake

Let your imagination run wild with fruity combinations to top this cake.

simple apple and blueberry cake

coconut french toast

*For the perfect drips of icing,
spoon it over chilled cakes.*

coconut cakes with dark chocolate glaze

chocolate and cinnamon wontons

16 wonton wrappers*
40g butter, melted
16 small squares (120g) dark chocolate*
1 teaspoon ground cinnamon
2 tablespoons caster (superfine) sugar

Preheat oven to 180°C (350°F). Brush the edges of the wonton wrappers with a little butter and place a chocolate square on one half of each wrapper. Fold over the wrappers to enclose and press to seal. Place on a baking tray lined with non-stick baking paper. Brush wontons with butter and sprinkle with combined cinnamon and sugar. Bake for 8 minutes or until golden. Serve warm. *Serves 4.*

ultimate one-bowl chocolate dessert cake

125g butter, chopped
375g dark chocolate*, coarsely chopped
1 cup (175g) brown sugar
¼ cup (35g) plain (all-purpose) flour, sifted
2 tablespoons milk
1 cup (120g) almond meal* (ground almonds)
5 eggs
cocoa, for dusting

Preheat oven to 170°C (325°F). Place the butter and chocolate in a bowl and either microwave in short bursts until melted or melt in a heatproof bowl over a saucepan of simmering water. Add the sugar, flour, milk and almond meal and mix to combine. Add the eggs and mix well. Pour mixture into a greased 22cm round springform tin lined with non-stick baking paper. Cover the tin with aluminium foil and bake for 40 minutes. Uncover and cool in the tin. Dust with cocoa and serve with cream and berries. *Serves 10.*

simple apple and blueberry cake

1½ cups (225g) self-raising (self-rising) flour, sifted
¾ cup (165g) caster (superfine) sugar
125g butter, softened
1 teaspoon vanilla extract
2 eggs
½ cup (125ml) milk
1 apple, cored and thinly sliced
¾ cup frozen or fresh blueberries
2 tablespoons demerara sugar*

Preheat oven to 160°C (325°F). Place flour, sugar, butter, vanilla, eggs and milk in the bowl of an electric mixer and beat until just combined. Spoon mixture into a greased 22cm springform tin lined with non-stick baking paper. Top with the apple and blueberries and sprinkle with sugar. Bake for 45 minutes or until the cake is cooked when tested with a skewer. Serve with vanilla ice-cream. *Serves 8–10.*

coconut french toast

4 thick slices white bread
50g dark chocolate*, melted
1 egg
½ cup (125ml) single (pouring) cream*
1 teaspoon vanilla extract
¼ cup (40g) icing (confectioner's) sugar, sifted
¾ cup (60g) desiccated coconut*
butter, for frying
icing (confectioner's) sugar, extra, to serve

Remove the crusts from the bread and cut each slice in half. Spread a little of the chocolate over half the bread slices and sandwich together with remaining halves. Whisk together the egg, cream, vanilla and sugar and place in a shallow dish. Dip the bread into the egg mixture for 30 seconds each side. Sprinkle each side of the bread with the coconut to coat. Heat a non-stick frying pan over medium-high heat. Add a little butter to the pan and swirl to melt. Add the bread and cook for 1–2 minutes each side or until golden. Dust with icing sugar and serve with ice-cream. *Serves 2–4.*

coconut cakes with dark chocolate glaze

125g butter, melted
1 cup (80g) desiccated coconut*
1⅔ cups (270g) icing (confectioner's) sugar, sifted
½ cup (75g) plain (all-purpose) flour, sifted
½ teaspoon baking powder
5 eggwhites
dark chocolate glaze
150g dark chocolate*, coarsely chopped
½ cup (125ml) single (pouring) cream*

Preheat oven to 180°C (350°F). Place the butter, coconut, sugar, flour, baking powder and eggwhites in a bowl and whisk to combine. Divide the mixture into a well-greased 12-hole ½-cup capacity (125ml) muffin tin or dariole moulds. Bake for 12–15 minutes or until just cooked in the centre when tested with a skewer. Stand the cakes for 2 minutes then remove from the tin and cool completely on wire racks. To make the dark chocolate glaze, place the chocolate and cream in a saucepan over low heat and stir until smooth. Cool the mixture until it is a thick icing consistency and spoon over the cooled cakes to serve. *Makes 12.*

Try other juices such as pineapple, cranberry or pink grapefruit.

blood orange granita

summer fruit crumbles

strawberry-maple tarte tatins

summer fruit crumbles

6 small plums, halved
1 peach, sliced
125g blueberries
125g raspberries
crumble topping
90g butter, chopped
½ cup (75g) plain (all-purpose) flour
⅓ cup (75g) caster (superfine) sugar
1 teaspoon ground cinnamon
¼ cup (35g) slivered almonds
ice-cream or double (thick) cream, to serve

Preheat oven to 200°C (400°F). Divide the fruit among 4 small ovenproof dishes. To make the crumble topping, place the butter, flour, sugar and cinnamon in a bowl. Rub the mixture with your fingertips until the butter is rubbed through. Stir through the almonds and spoon on top of the fruit. Bake for 20 minutes or until the crumble is golden and the fruit is soft. Serve warm or cold with ice-cream or double cream. *Serves 4.*

lemon puddings

blood orange granita

1⅓ cups (330ml) water
1 cup (220g) caster (superfine) sugar
2 cups (500ml) blood orange juice

Place the water and sugar in a saucepan over low heat and stir until sugar dissolves. Set aside to cool. Combine the sugar syrup with the juice and pour into a metal container. Freeze the juice mixture for 4 hours or until set. To serve, rake the granita with a fork and spoon into serving glasses. *Serves 4.*

strawberry-maple tarte tatins

18 strawberries, hulled
¼ cup (60ml) maple syrup
1 x 200g sheet store-bought puff pastry*, thawed

Preheat oven to 200°C (400°F). Place 3 strawberries in each of 6 holes of a ½-cup capacity (125ml) non-stick muffin pan. Pour the syrup over the strawberries. Cut 6 x 12cm circles from the pastry and place on top of the strawberries. Bake for 15–20 minutes or until the pastry is puffed and golden. Stand for 8 minutes then invert the tarts onto serving plates. Serve with double (thick) cream. *Serves 6.*

For a more wintry dessert, you could top the tarts with thin slices of apple or firm brown pear instead.

lemon pudding

2 cups (500ml) single (pouring) cream*
½ cup (110g) caster (superfine) sugar
⅓ cup (80ml) lemon juice
raspberries, to serve

Place the cream and sugar in a saucepan over medium heat and bring to a simmer, stirring occasionally. Allow to simmer for 6 minutes or until the cream has reduced slightly. Add the lemon juice and simmer for a further 2 minutes. Pour into 4 x ¾-cup (180ml) capacity cups, glasses or ramekins and refrigerate until set. Serve with fresh raspberries. *Serves 4.*

This creamy and velvety lemon dessert is so easy to make and thickens as if by magic.

cheat's caramel ice-cream

600ml single (pouring) cream*
1 x 340g can caramel or dulce de leche*

Place the cream in a bowl and whisk until soft peaks have almost formed. Mix the caramel until smooth and fold into the cream. Place in a metal container and cover. Freeze for 3–4 hours or until firm. Serve in scoops. *Serves 4–6.*

cheat's caramel ice-cream

chocolate pots

Don't just save this for dessert;
it also makes for a very decadent
weekend brunch.

baked ricotta with vanilla honey

chocolate pots

125g dark chocolate*, coarsely chopped
1 cup (250ml) single (pouring) cream*
2 tablespoons coffee or chocolate liqueur
thin biscuits or wafers, to serve

Place the chocolate and cream in a saucepan over low heat and stir until melted and smooth. Remove from heat and stir through the liqueur. Pour into small glasses and refrigerate until cold. Serve with thin crisp biscuits, such as almond bread. *Serves 4.*

Use your favourite liqueur in this recipe to suit your own taste.

baked ricotta with vanilla honey

500g ricotta
⅓ cup (115g) honey
1 teaspoon vanilla bean paste*
fruit toast, to serve

Preheat oven to 160°C (325°F). Firmly press the ricotta into 4 x ½-cup capacity (125ml) dariole moulds and place on a baking tray. Bake for 25 minutes and stand for 2 minutes before turning out onto a baking tray lined with non-stick baking paper. Preheat the grill to high. Combine the honey and vanilla and spoon some of the honey mixture over the ricotta to coat. Grill for 10 minutes, then spoon over more honey mixture and grill for a further 5 minutes. Baste with the honey in the pan and grill for a further 5 minutes or until the ricotta is golden. Serve with thin slices of toasted fruit bread. *Serves 4.*

lemon yoghurt cake

¾ cup (180ml) vegetable oil
2 eggs
1 tablespoon finely grated lemon rind
2 tablespoons lemon juice
1 cup (280g) thick natural yoghurt
1¾ cups (385g) caster (superfine) sugar
2 cups (300g) self-raising (self-rising) flour
lemon frosting
¾ cup (120g) granulated sugar
¼ cup (60ml) lemon juice

Preheat oven to 180°C (350°F). Place the oil, eggs, rind, lemon juice, yoghurt and sugar in a bowl and whisk to combine. Sift over the flour and stir until smooth. Pour the mixture into a greased 24cm fluted ring tin and bake for 35 minutes or until cooked when tested with a skewer. While the cake is still hot remove from the tin and place on a plate. To make the lemon frosting, gently stir together the sugar and lemon juice. Spoon over the cake and allow to set. Serve warm. *Serves 10–12.*

The hot cake sets this simple icing to an amazing tangy, crystalised crust. Just try stopping at one piece.

lemon yoghurt cake

style

I'm often asked where I find my inspiration. It's in the little details. A tiny embellishment here or there, a quirky twist on typography or a design... I take the same approach to presenting food. It's about small details to bring your tabletop to life. Here are some simple ideas to frame your culinary creations and take the stress out of entertaining.

Who doesn't like a lollipop?
These macaron versions make a
chic place setting or centrepiece.

macaron lollipops

cool ending

A sweet way to let all the boys
and girls know where to be seated.

his and hers

good fortune

a picnic under wraps

a sweet for the road

macaron lollipops

These macaron lollipops are so simple to make. Use them as a place setting with a name tag attached, as a centrepiece piled high on the table or in a bowl or as a party favour for your next soirée or wedding. Simply insert a cardboard pop stick into each store-bought macaron. Slide them into a Cellophane bag and tie with ribbon or twine.

cool ending

There is nothing quite like a grown-up version of one of your childhood favourites. Freeze sophisticated flavours such as pomegranate, blood orange, pink grapefruit, lime and lychee in popsicle moulds. On a hot summer's day there is no better way to end a meal or send your guests on their way than with an ultra cool treat.

For a grown-up version, add a dash of white spirit to the popsicle mixture. Vodka and pink grapefruit, anyone?

his and hers

Solve the age-old problem of where to sit all the boys and girls. Make or buy sugar snap cookies flavoured as you please – my favourite is vanilla or cinnamon – and tie a small luggage tag to the cookie so you have a place to write a name. Guests can nibble on them with coffee at the end of the meal or slip them into little bags as a take-home sweet. If you run out of time, store-bought gingerbread men or any other cute cookies you can find will suffice.

good fortune

Let everyone at your next gathering enjoy their perfect tailor-made fortune, like a little piece of magic. Cut strips of paper and create your own personalised fortune for each guest. You can remove the existing fortune in a fortune cookie with thin tweezers if you are nimble enough, otherwise it's double the fun! These are also an easy way to make a named place setting for a dinner party or pile them in a bowl on the table for a great centrepiece.

a picnic under wraps

Whether it's a picnic or an outdoor feast, it's easy to keep it glam and organised when each guest has their own little picnic set under wraps, ready to dine. Wrap everything your guests need from a plate, cup, cutlery and straw in an oversized napkin to generously cover laps.

a sweet for the road

Make your favourite sweet desserts portable by arranging them in small jars. Attach a wooden spoon to make it a true portable eat-anywhere treat. Use them for picnics or for feeding large crowds at a buffet-type arrangement. They are also fun take-home gifts for your guests to share on their journey home. See pages 53 and 57 for a portable pavlova and berry trifle.

For a cute portable dessert, layer crushed meringues in a glass with fresh cream and your favourite fruit.

pretty pots

dinner station

pass the parcel

Plant your favourite herbs in painted recycled tins for a centrepiece with a difference... you can eat it!

green power

Say goodbye to soggy salads and hello to these clever individual ones you can dress at the table.

pretty pots

Turn old glass jars into pretty flower pots. Take a plain recycled jar and some paper or fabric offcuts and transform the jar into a stylish vessel for flowers to make a centrepiece or add a colourful touch to a sideboard. Choose seasonal colours or patterns to wrap the jars.

dinner station

Keep the stress levels low when you're casually entertaining by providing your guests with the flavours, ingredients and condiments they need to tailor-make their own gourmet burger or steak sandwich. Build a little station with all their needs. See pages 23, 72 and 155 for some inspiration.

pass the parcel

After choosing the menu, most people's main source of stress at a dinner party is how to get everything on the table as close to hot as possible. These individual paper parcels mean you're in with a chance. Make parcels of vegetable sides using seasonal vegies and flavour them with ingredients like lemon, fresh herbs, butter and salt and pepper. Bake the parcels until the vegetables are tender and either place them on a platter in the middle of the table or slide onto individual serving plates. The parcels keep your vegetables warm.

Assemble the parcels ahead of time and then just slide them in the oven when you're ready. Too easy.

green power

To create a quirky centrepiece, plant your favourite herbs in recycled tins sprayed in coordinating colours. Your guests can snip off fresh herbs to add to their dishes. After you've used them, you can keep them on the window sill or plant them in the garden.

individual salads

I'm not a huge fan of passing around an enormous salad bowl to feed a crowded table. Someone is always stuck with the soggy bits at the bottom! I like to make small individual bowls of salad ahead of time and place the dressing in small juice bottles for guests to dress their own at the table, so salads stay crisp.

crafty cartons

The humble egg carton comes into its own as a great carrier of small treats. They're great for mini muffins, mini cupcakes, chocolate truffles and other small sweet treats. Your little sweets will always arrive safely at your destination. See my too-easy blueberry muffin recipe on page 122.

The only problem with the perfect dozen — eager guests will notice any missing morsels!

have salad, will travel

The crunch and texture of a salad or the wonderful layers of a sandwich are often lost in transportation. The solution is to assemble a salad in layers either in individual jars or a large container and take the dressing separately to dress the salad just before serving. Guests can help themselves to a jar, add the dressing and gently shake or turn the jar to combine. You can also take sandwich fillings this way to a picnic and assemble into the bread on arrival.

This is great for a party or picnic. You can make the salad ahead while maintaining maximum crunch and texture without compromising on style.

the perfect cut

There are so many different ways to present food but often the simplest are the best. This is my favourtite food styling rule. By cutting baby lettuce hearts in half, they not only look amazing but they also make it easy for dressing to form little puddles between the layers, making your salad perfectly dressed from start to finish.

host with the most

I really appreciate an invitation to dinner and like to bring a little gift for the host or hostess, making sure I'm invited back! I make a hot chocolate mix of dark chocolate chopped in the food processor with a few tablespoons of cocoa for extra richness, balanced with a few tablespoons of icing sugar. My other favourite is to make a simple hand scrub from course salt and equal measures of lemon juice and olive oil. It's great to remove any kitchen smells, such as garlic or onion, from hands while keeping them soft.

tea time

A special way to end a meal is with a fresh tea. Make your own combinations using herbs, spices or citrus. I like to use cinnamon, lemon, ginger and mint. For a warmer, spicier version, you could use vanilla bean and star anise. Simply tie your choice of ingredients into a square of muslin and steep in cups or a teapot for 4–5 minutes. Add sugar if desired and enjoy.

A selection of fresh homemade tea bags makes for a perfectly chic finish.

You don't need to reinvent the wheel when it comes to plating food. Simply cut it a little differently.

the perfect cut

have salad, will travel

host with the most

tea time

DOUBLE BAY
DOVER HEIGHTS
EDDY AV. CENT. RAILWAY
EDGECLIFF
ELIZABETH BAY
ERSKINEVILLE
EXPRESS
FLOWER AND STOREY STS
FOVEAUX ST. CENT. RAILWAY
FRANKLIN ST. MALABAR

glossary & measures

Wherever possible, I've tried to source most of the ingredients in this book from supermarkets. However, if you're unsure of a particular item, this glossary will help. Ingredients marked with an asterisk have a glossary entry. There's also a useful list of global measures, temperatures and common conversions to help you follow the recipes easily.

aïoli
Garlic-flavoured mayonnaise.

almonds

meal
Also known as ground almonds, almond meal is available from most supermarkets. Used instead of, or as well as, flour in cakes and desserts. Make your own by processing whole skinned almonds to a fine meal in a food processor or blender (125g almonds will give 1 cup almond meal). To remove the skins from almonds, soak in boiling water, then using your fingers, slip the skins off.

slivered
Skinned almonds cut in small pieces lengthways and used as a topping in baking and sprinkling for salads.

flaked
Skinned almonds cut into paper-thin slices.

blanching
A cooking method used to slightly soften the texture, heighten the colour and enhance the flavour of food such as vegetables. Plunge the ingredient briefly into boiling unsalted water, then remove and refresh under cold water. Drain well before using in salads or as a garnish.

blood orange
An almost seedless citrus with red-streaked rind and flesh and sweet, non-acidic deep raspberry red juice.

broccolini
A cross between gai larn (Chinese broccoli) and broccoli, this green vegetable has long, thin stems and small florets. Sold in bunches, it can be substituted for broccoli.

butter
Unless stated otherwise in a recipe, butter should be at room temperature for cooking. It should not be half-melted or too soft to handle, but should still have some 'give' when pressed. When using butter for pastry, it should be cold and chopped into small pieces so that it can be evenly distributed through the flour. Salted butter has a longer refrigerator shelf life, which makes it preferable for some people.

butter beans
Large, plump white beans also known as lima beans. They go well in soups, stews and salads. Available from delicatessens and supermarkets either canned or in dried form. Dried beans need to be soaked overnight in water before cooking.

buttermilk
Originally the name given to the slightly tangy liquid which was left over when cream was separated from milk, these days buttermilk is manufactured by adding cultures to low- or no-fat milk. Buttermilk is used in sauces, dressings and baked items.

cannellini or white beans
These small, kidney-shaped beans are available from supermarkets either canned or in dried form. Dried beans need to be soaked overnight in water before cooking.

capers
Capers are the small, green flower buds of the caper bush. Available packed either in brine or salt. Use salt-packed capers when possible, as the texture is firmer and the flavour superior. Before use, rinse thoroughly, drain and pat dry.

capsicum (bell pepper)
A versatile fruit from the solanaceae (nightshade) family, the capsicum is available in red, green, yellow and orange varieties. It can be eaten raw in salads or roasted and cooked in stir-fries, stews and sauces or made into a spicy condiment.

celeriac (celery root)
A root vegetable with white flesh and a mild celery flavour. It is available in winter from supermarkets and greengrocers. Use in salads and soups or roast it with meats.

caramelised onion
Sliced onion cooked slowly to release all its sugars and made even more intense in flavour by the addition of brown sugar and balsamic vinegar.

cheese

blue
The distinctive veins and flavour of blue cheeses are achieved by adding a cultured mould. Most have a crumbly texture and acidic taste, which becomes rounded and more mellow with age.

bocconcini
Small, bite-sized balls of mozzarella.

cheddar
A firm cow's milk cheese with a sharp taste and crumbly texture. Originally from south-west England, cheddar is now one of the world's most popular cheeses.

feta
Made from goat's, sheep's or cow's milk, feta is a salty, crumbly cheese, which is frequently stored in brine to extend its shelf life. It's an essential of the Greek kitchen.

goat's cheese & curd
Goat's milk has a tart flavour, so cheese made from it, sometimes labelled chèvre, has a sharp, slightly acidic taste. Immature goat's cheese is milder and creamier than mature cheese and is sometimes found labelled as goat's curd.

gorgonzola
Blue cheese of Italian origin. Dolce refers to an extra creamy sweet version.

haloumi
Firm white Cypriot cheese made from sheep's milk. It has a stringy texture and is usually sold in brine. Available from delicatessens and some supermarkets. Holds its shape during grilling and frying, so is ideal for kebabs.

labne
Middle Eastern cheese made from strained yoghurt based on cow's milk.

manchego
Firm ivory-yellow cheese of Spanish origin made from sheep's milk.

mascarpone
A fresh Italian triple-cream, curd-style cheese. It has a similar consistency to thick (double) cream and is often used in the same way. Available in tubs from speciality food stores and supermarkets, it's used in sauces and desserts such as tiramisu.

mozzarella

Italian in origin, mozzarella is the mild cheese of pizza, lasagne and tomato salads. It's made by cutting and spinning (or stringing) the curd to achieve a smooth, elastic consistency. The most prized variety is made from buffalo milk. Bocconcini are small, bite-sized balls of mozzarella.

parmesan

Italy's favourite hard, granular cheese is made from cow's milk. Parmigiano reggiano is the 'Rolls Royce' variety, made under strict guidelines in the Emilia-Romagna region and aged for an average of two years. Grana padano mainly comes from Lombardy and is aged for 15 months.

ricotta

A creamy, finely grained white cheese. Ricotta means 'recooked' in Italian, a reference to the way the cheese is produced by heating the whey left over from making other cheese varieties. It's fresh and creamy and low in fat.

stilton

Britain's favourite blue cheese with a strong flavour and deep veins.

taleggio

Washed rind Italian cheese with a strong aroma but mild flavour.

chervil

A herb relative of parsley with a slightly aniseed flavour and aroma.

chickpea (garbanzo)

A legume native from western Asia across the Mediterranean, the chickpea is used in soups, stews and is the base ingredient in the Middle Eastern dip called hummus. Dried chickpeas must be soaked before cooking, but you can also buy them canned. Drain and rinse the canned variety before incorporating them into dishes.

chilli jam

Thai condiment made from ginger, chilli, garlic and shrimp paste used in soups and stir-fries. It goes well with roasted meats, egg dishes and cheese and is often served in a dollop as a garnish.

chinese five-spice

A blend of cinnamon, Sichuan pepper, star anise, clove and fennel seeds. Available at Asian food stores and supermarkets.

chinese rice wine or shaoxing

Similar to dry sherry, Shaoxing or Chinese cooking wine is a blend of glutinous rice, millet, a special yeast and the local spring waters of Shao Hsing, where it is made, in northern China. It is sold in the Asian aisle of your supermarket and in Asian grocery stores, often labelled 'shao hsing'.

chorizo

Firm, spicy, coarse-textured Spanish pork sausage seasoned with pepper, paprika and chillies. Available from some butchers and most delicatessens.

coconut

cream

The cream that rises to the top after the first pressing of coconut milk, coconut cream is a rich, sweet liquid that is both higher in energy and fat than regular coconut milk. Sold in cans at the supermarket. Light (low-fat) versions are also available.

desiccated

Dried fine flakes of coconut flesh usually used in baking.

milk

A milky sweet white liquid made by soaking grated fresh coconut flesh or desiccated coconut in warm water and squeezing through muslin or cheesecloth to extract the liquid. Available in cans or freeze-dried from supermarkets, coconut milk should not be confused with coconut juice, which is a clear liquid found inside young coconuts and often served as a refreshing drink in Asia.

coriander (cilantro)

Also known as Chinese parsley, this pungent green herb is common in Asian and Mexican cooking. The finely chopped roots are sometimes incorporated in curry pastes. The dried seeds are an Indian staple, sold ground or whole and one of the base ingredients in curry powder. The dried form can not be substituted for fresh leaves.

couscous

The name given to both the national dish of Algeria, Tunisia and Morocco and the tiny grains of flour-coated semolina that make it.

cream

The fat content determines the names of the different types of cream and their uses.

crème fraîche

A fermented cream with a minimum fat content of 35 per cent and a tangy flavour.

double (heavy)

Has a butter fat content of 40–50 per cent. It is sometimes called pure cream and is usually served on the side.

single (pouring)

Has a butter fat content of 20–30 per cent. It is the type of cream most commonly used for making ice-cream, panna cotta and custard. It can be whipped to a light and airy consistency and served on the side.

sour

A thick, commercially cultured cream with a minimum fat content of 35 per cent.

thickened

This is single (pouring) cream that has had a vegetable gum added to stabilise it. The gum makes the cream a little thicker and easier to whip. It's ideal for desserts and pavlovas.

dijon mustard

Also known as French mustard, this is a pale, creamy and fairly mild-flavoured mustard.

dulce de leche

This is a thick milk caramel made from slowly heating and thickening sweetened milk. You can buy it in cans or make your own by boiling an unopened can of sweetened condensed milk for 2–3 hours. It's used in desserts.

eggs

The standard egg size used in this book is 60g. It is important to use the right size eggs for a recipe, as this will affect the outcome of baked goods. The correct volume is especially important when using eggwhites to make meringues. You should use eggs at room temperature for baking.

eschalots (shallots)

A member of the onion family, eschalots are smaller and have a milder flavour than brown, red or white onions. A popular ingredient in Europe, they look like small elongated brown onions with purple-grey tinged skins. Asian shallots are smaller again, with pinkish skins and grow in small clusters. They're used in curry pastes.

fennel

With a mild aniseed flavour and crisp texture, fennel bulb is ideal for salads or roasting with meat and fish. It is available from supermarkets and greengrocers.

flour

Made from ground cereal grains, flour is the primary ingredient in breads, cakes and many other baked goods including biscuits, pastries, pizzas and pie cases.

cornflour (cornstarch)

When made from ground corn or maize, cornflour is a gluten-free flour. It is often blended with water or stock to use as a thickening agent. Not to be confused with cornflour in the United States, which is finely ground corn meal used for making tortillas.

plain (all-purpose)

Ground from the endosperm of wheat, plain white flour contains no raising agent.

self-raising (self-rising)

Ground from the endosperm of wheat, self-raising flour contains raising agents including sodium carbonates and calcium phosphates. To make it using plain flour add 2 teaspoons of baking powder for every 250g of flour.

rice

A fine flour made from ground white rice. Used as a thickening agent, in baking and to coat foods when cooking Asian dishes, particularly those needing a crispy finish. Buy from supermarkets.

frisée (curly endive)

This curly-leafed salad green with a slightly bitter flavour is a popular accompaniment to salads containing poached eggs.

gai larn (chinese broccoli)

Also known as Chinese broccoli or Chinese kale, gai larn is a leafy vegetable with dark green leaves, small flowers and stout stems.

gelatine

Available as a powder or in leaf form, gelatine is a thickening agent made from collagen. It must be dissolved in warm water before being added to the recipe. Agar-agar is a vegetarian alternative.

gowgee wrappers

Chinese in origin, these square thin sheets of dough are available fresh or frozen. They can be steamed or fried. Fill them with meat and vegetables to make dumplings for soup or use as a crunchy base for nibbles, or deep-fry and sprinkle with sugar for dessert.

green mango

Green version of the tropical fruit with a strong sour taste, used in Asian salads.

green onion (scallion)

Both the white and green part of this small bulbed, mild onion are used in salads, as a garnish and in Asian cooking.

harissa

A North African condiment, harissa is a hot red paste made from chilli, garlic and spices including coriander, caraway and cumin. May also contain tomato. Available in jars and tubes from supermarkets and speciality food stores, harissa enlivens tagines and couscous dishes and can be added to dressings and sauces for an instant flavour kick. You can also use it in a marinade for meats.

kaffir lime leaves

Fragrant leaves with a distinctive, double-leaf structure, used crushed or shredded in Thai dishes. Available fresh or dried from Asian food stores.

lemongrass

A tall, lemon-scented grass used in Asian cooking, and particularly in Thai dishes. Peel away the outer leaves and chop the tender white root-end finely, or add in large pieces during cooking and remove before serving. If adding in large pieces, bruise them with the back of a large knife.

maple syrup

A sweetener made from the sap of the maple tree. Be sure to use pure maple syrup rather than imitation or pancake syrup, which is made from corn syrup flavoured with maple and lacks the flavour of the real thing.

mirin

A Japanese pale yellow cooking wine made from glutinous rice and alcohol. Sweet mirin is flavoured with corn syrup.

miso paste

A traditional Japanese ingredient produced by fermenting rice, barley or soybeans, with salt and fungus to a thick paste. Used for sauces and spreads, pickling vegetables or meats, and mixing with dashi soup stock to serve as miso soup. Red miso paste is robust while white miso paste is more delicate in flavour. Available from supermarkets and Asian food stores.

noodles

Keep a supply of dried noodles in the pantry for last-minute meals. Fresh noodles will keep in the fridge for a week. Available from supermarkets and Asian food stores.

cellophane (bean thread)

Also called mung bean vermicelli or glass noodles, these noodles are very thin and almost transparent. Soak them in boiling water and drain well to prepare for use.

dried rice

Fine, dry noodles that are common in Southeast Asian cooking. Depending on their thickness, rice noodles need only be boiled briefly, or soaked in hot water until pliable. Sometimes called rice stick noodles.

shanghai

Chinese wheat noodles available dried and fresh in a variety of thicknesses. Fresh noodles need to be soaked in hot water or cooked in boiling water. Dried noodles should be boiled before use.

soba

Japanese noodles made from buckwheat and wheat flour, soba are greyish brown in colour and served in both hot and cold savoury dishes.

udon
Japanese thick white wheat flour noodles, popular in soups and braised dishes.

olives

black
Black olives are more mature and less salty than the green variety. Choose firm olives with good colour and a fruity taste.

ligurian/wild
Usually labelled or sold as Ligurian olives, wild olives are uncultivated and grow close to the ground in clusters. This small variety of olive can range in colour from pale mustard to dark purple and black. The thin flesh has a nutty flavour that makes them a great substitute for peanuts. Niçoise olives are similar in size as well as flavour.

kalamata
Of Greek origin, the large Kalamata olives have an intense flavour, which makes them the ideal choice for Greek salads. They are sometimes sold split to better absorb the flavour of the oil in which they are stored.

oil
Olive oil is graded according to its flavour, aroma and acidity. Extra virgin is the highest quality oil; it contains no more than 1 per cent acid. Virgin is the next best; it contains 1.5 per cent or less acid and may have a slightly fruitier taste than extra virgin. Bottles labelled 'olive oil' contain a combination of refined and unrefined virgin olive oil. Light olive oil is the least pure in quality and intensity of flavour; it is not lower in fat. Colours vary from deep green through to gold and very light yellow.

tapenade
Paste made by blending olives, capers, garlic and anchovies with oil. Served as a dip with crackers, or spread on bruschetta and pizzas, it makes a good marinade and partner for cold meat or cheeses.

pancetta
A cured and rolled Italian-style meat that is like prosciutto but less salty and with a softer texture. It's sold in chunks or thinly sliced and can be eaten uncooked or used in pasta sauces and risottos.

paprika
Spice made from ground, dried capsicum. Originally from Hungary, it comes in mild (sweet), and a hot (smoked) Spanish version. Adds flavour and vibrant colour to meat and rice dishes.

pasta

fettuccine
Ribbon pasta available fresh and dried.

orecchiette
Small disc-shaped pasta that gets its name from the Italian for 'little ears'.

pappardelle
Thick ribbon pasta available fresh and dried.

penne
Pasta tubes, sometimes with a serrated edge.

rigatoni
Large grooved tube-shaped pasta.

spaghetti
Long thin strands of pasta available fresh and dried.

pastry

filo
Extremely thin sheets of pastry popular in Greek, Turkish and Middle Eastern baking, particularly for sweets.

puff
This pastry is time-consuming and quite difficult to make, so many cooks opt to use store-bought puff pastry. It can be bought in blocks from pâtisseries or bought in both block and sheet forms from supermarkets. You may need to layer several sheets of puff pastry together to make a thicker crown. It's perfect for quick tarts or desserts.

shortcrust
A savoury or sweet pastry that is available ready-made in blocks and frozen sheets. Keep a supply for last-minute pies or make your own pastry:

1½ cups (225g) plain (all-purpose) flour
125g butter, chilled and cut into cubes
3 egg yolks
1 tablespoon iced water

Place the flour and butter in the bowl of a food processor and process in short bursts until mixture resembles fine breadcrumbs. While the motor is running, add the egg yolks and water. Process until the dough just comes together. Turn dough out onto a lightly floured surface and gently bring together to form a ball. Using your hands, flatten dough into a disk. Wrap in plastic wrap and refrigerate. When ready to use, roll out on a lightly floured surface to 3mm thick. To make sweet shortcrust pastry, add ½ cup (80g) icing (confectioner's) sugar.

pistachio
A green delicately flavoured nut inside a hard outer shell. Used in Middle Eastern cuisine, salads and baking.

polenta
Used extensively in northern Italy, this corn meal is cooked in simmering water until it has a porridge-like consistency. In this form it is enriched with butter or cheese and served with meat dishes. Otherwise it is left to cool, cut into squares and grilled, fried or baked. Instant polenta is made from precooked corn meal and is ready in 5 minutes.

pomegranate
The bright red fruit of a tropical bush is packed with seeds surrounded by little sackfuls of astringent juice. The seeds make a great garnish or salad ingredient. To extract the juice, roll the fruit on a bench, halve and squeeze with a citrus juicer. Molasses is a thick dark syrup made from the juice.

porcini mushrooms
Available fresh in Europe and the UK and sold dried elsewhere, including Australia and the US. They have an almost meaty texture and earthy taste. Soak dried porcini mushrooms before using, and use the soaking liquid if desired.

preserved lemon
Preserved lemons are rubbed with salt, packed in jars, covered with lemon juice and left for about four weeks. They're often flavoured with cloves, cinnamon or chilli. Remove the flesh, rinse and chop the rind for use in cooking. Available from delicatessens and speciality food stores.

prosciutto
Italian ham that's been salted and dried for up to two years. The paper-thin slices are eaten raw or used to lend their distinctive flavour to braises and other cooked dishes. Often used to wrap figs or melon as part of an antipasto platter.

quince paste
Also known as membrillo for its Spanish origins, this intensely aromatic paste is made by boiling quinces, lemon juice and sugar to a thick condiment that teams well with roasted meats, cheeses and nuts.

rice
arborio
Risotto rice with a short, plump-looking grain. It has surface starch which creates a cream with the stock when cooked to al dente. Substitute with carnaroli, roma, baldo, padano, vialone or Calriso rice.

basmati
Long-grain, aromatic white rice.

jasmine
Sometimes called Thai rice, a long-grain white rice with a delicate floral flavour.

red curry paste
Buy good-quality pastes in jars from Asian food stores or the supermarket. When trying a new brand, it is a good idea to add a little at a time to test the heat as the chilli intensity can vary significantly from brand to brand.

rocket (arugula)
A tangy, peppery salad leaf popular in Mediterranean cuisines, rocket makes a classic Italian salad with pear and parmesan, and also makes a great pesto to serve on bruschetta, in soups and as a dip.

rosewater
An essence distilled from rose petals, rosewater is one of the cornerstone flavours of Indian, Middle Eastern and Turkish tables. It's the distinctive flavour in Turkish delight.

sauces
fish
An amber-coloured liquid drained from salted, fermented fish and used to add flavour to Thai and Vietnamese dishes. Available from supermarkets and Asian food stores, it's often labelled 'nam pla'.

hoisin
A thick, sweet Chinese sauce made from fermented soybeans, sugar, salt and red rice. Used as a dipping sauce or marinade and as the sauce for Peking duck, hoisin is available in supermarkets.

oyster
A viscous dark brown sauce commonly used in Asian stir-fries, soups and hotpots, oyster sauce is made from oysters, brine and flavour enhancers, which are boiled until reduced to a thick, caramelised, flavour-packed sauce.

worcestershire
A thin, dark brown sauce developed by the British in India, with strong overtones of tamarind and spice. Used to give a kick to soups, stews and oysters Kilpatrick.

sesame seeds
These small seeds have a strong nutty flavour. White sesame seeds are the most common variety, but black, or unhulled, seeds are popular for coatings in Asian cooking. Sesame oil is made by extracting the oil from roasted seeds while tahini is a paste made from crushed seeds.

sponge finger biscuits
Sweet and light Italian finger-shaped biscuits, also known as savoiardi. Great for desserts such as tiramisu because they absorb other flavours and soften well, yet at the same time maintain their shape. These biscuits are available in large and small versions from most supermarkets.

sugar
Extracted as crystals from the juice of the sugar cane plant or beet, sugar is a sweetener, flavour enhancer, bulking agent and preservative.

brown
Processed with molasses. It comes in differing shades of brown, according to the quantity of molasses added, which varies between countries. This also affects the taste of the sugar, and therefore the end product. Brown sugar is sometimes called light brown sugar. You can substitute dark brown sugar for more intense flavour.

caster (superfine)
Gives baked products a light texture and crumb, which is important for many cakes and light desserts such as meringues.

demerara
Small-grained, golden coloured crystal sugar used in baking.

granulated
Regular sugar is used in baking when a light texture is not crucial. The crystals are large, so you need to beat, add liquids or heat regular sugar to dissolve it.

icing (confectioner's)
Regular granulated sugar ground to a very fine powder. It often clumps together and needs to be sieved before using. Use pure icing sugar not icing sugar mixture, which contains cornflour (cornstarch) and needs more liquid.

star anise
Small, brown seed-cluster that is shaped like a star. It has a strong aniseed flavour that can be used whole or ground in sweet and savoury dishes. Available from supermarkets and speciality food stores.

sumac
Dried berries of a flowering plant are ground to produce an acidic, reddish-purple powder popular in the Middle East.

sweet potato
Long, tuberous root available in white- and orange-fleshed varieties. The orange sweet potato, also known as kumara, is sweeter and moister than the white. Both varieties can be roasted, boiled or mashed. Although different from the yam, they can be cooked in a similar manner.

tahini
A thick paste made from ground sesame seeds. Used in Middle Eastern cooking, it is available in jars and cans from supermarkets and health food shops. It is used to make the popular dip called hummus.

tarragon

Called the king of herbs by the French and used in many of their classic sauces such as Bearnaise and tartare. It has a slightly aniseed flavour.

tins

Aluminium (aluminum) tins are fine but stainless steel will last longer and won't warp or buckle. Always measure widths across the base of the tin.

muffin

The standard sizes are a 12-hole tin, each hole with ½ cup (125ml) capacity, or a 6-hole tin, each hole with 1 cup (250ml) capacity. Mini-muffin tins have a capacity of 1½ tablespoons. Non-stick tins make for easy removal, or line with paper patty cases.

round

The standard sizes for round springform tins are 18cm, 20cm, 22cm and 24cm. The 20cm and 24cm tins are must-haves.

springform

The standard sizes for round tins are 18cm, 20cm, 22cm and 24cm. The 20cm and 24cm round tins are the must-have members of the range.

square

The standard sizes for square tins are 18cm, 20cm, 22cm and 24cm. If you have a recipe for a cake cooked in a round tin and you want to use a square tin, the general rule is to subtract 2cm from the size of the tin. You would need a 20cm square tin for a recipe calling for a 22cm round cake tin.

tofu

Literally translated as 'bean curd', tofu is a high-protein food popular across Asia. Made by coagulating the milk of soy beans, and pressing the curd into blocks, tofu comes in several grades according to the amount of moisture which has been removed. Silken tofu is the softest, with a custard-like texture. Soft tofu is slightly firmer, while dried or firm tofu has the texture of, and cuts like, a semi-hard cheese such as haloumi. Usually sold packed in water from the refrigerated section of supermarkets and Asian food stores.

tomato

bottled tomato pasta sauce

Sometimes labeled 'passata' or 'sugo'. Italian for 'passed', passata is made by removing the skins and seeds from ripe tomatoes and passing the flesh through a sieve to make a thick, rich, pulpy tomato purée. Sugo is made from crushed tomatoes so it has a little more texture than passata. Both are available in bottles from supermarkets and are essential to the Italian table.

paste

Triple concentrated tomato purée used to flavour soups, sauces and stews.

purée

Canned puréed tomatoes (not tomato paste). Substitute with fresh or canned peeled and puréed tomatoes.

sun-dried

Tomato pieces that have been dried with salt which dehydrates the fruit and concentrates the flavour. Available plain or packed in oil.

tzatziki

Greek dip made from thick natural yoghurt, garlic and chopped or grated cucumber, sometimes with dill added. Available in supermarkets, it can also be used as a sauce for grilled meat and seafood or served as an accompaniment to savoury pastries.

vanilla beans

These cured pods from the vanilla orchid are used whole, and often split with the tiny seeds scraped into the mixture, to infuse flavour into custard and cream-based recipes. If unavailable, substitute 1 vanilla bean with 1 teaspoon pure vanilla extract (a dark, thick liquid – not essence) or store-bought vanilla bean paste.

vanilla extract

For a pure vanilla taste, use a good-quality vanilla extract, not an essence or imitation flavour, or use a vanilla bean.

vinegar

balsamic

Originally from Modena in Italy, there are many varieties on the market ranging in quality and flavour. Aged balsamics are generally preferable. Also available in a milder, white version which is used in dishes where the colour is important.

balsamic glaze

Reduction of balsamic vinegar and sugar.

malt

A brown vinegar made from fermented malt and beech shavings.

rice wine

Made from fermenting rice or rice wine, rice vinegar is milder and sweeter than vinegars made by oxidising distilled alcohol or wine made from grapes. Rice wine vinegar is available in white (colourless to pale yellow), black and red varieties from Asian food stores and some supermarkets.

white wine

Made from distilled white wine.

water chestnuts

Edible corms of a water-growing sedge that are popular for their crunchy texture in Chinese cuisine. They're great in stir-fries.

wasabi

Wasabi is a very hot Japanese horseradish paste used in making sushi and as a condiment. Available from Asian food stores and supermarkets.

wonton wrappers

Chinese in origin, these square thin sheets of dough are available fresh or frozen. They can be steamed or fried. Fill them with meat and vegetables to make dumplings for soup or use as a crunchy base for nibbles, or deep-fry or bake and sprinkle with sugar for dessert.

za'atar

Middle Eastern spice mix containing dried herbs, sesame seeds and sumac. Often used as a crust for grilled and baked meat.

global measures

measures vary from Europe
to the US and even from
Australia to NZ.

metric & imperial

Measuring cups and spoons may vary
slightly from one country to another,
but the difference is generally not
sufficient to affect a recipe. All cup and
spoon measures are level. An Australian
measuring cup holds 250ml (8 fl oz).

One Australian metric teaspoon holds
5ml, one Australian tablespoon holds
20ml (4 teaspoons). However, in North
America, New Zealand and the UK they
use 15ml (3-teaspoon) tablespoons.

When measuring liquid ingredients
remember that 1 American pint contains
500ml (16 fl oz), but 1 Imperial pint
contains 600ml (20 fl oz).

When measuring dry ingredients, add
the ingredient loosely to the cup and
level with a knife. Don't tap or shake
to compact the ingredient unless
the recipe requests 'firmly packed'.

liquids & solids

measuring cups and spoons
and a set of scales are great
assets in the kitchen.

liquids

cup	metric	imperial
⅛ cup	30ml	1 fl oz
¼ cup	60ml	2 fl oz
⅓ cup	80ml	2½ fl oz
½ cup	125ml	4 fl oz
⅔ cup	160ml	5 fl oz
¾ cup	180ml	6 fl oz
1 cup	250ml	8 fl oz
2 cups	500ml	16 fl oz
2¼ cups	600ml	20 fl oz
4 cups	1 litre	32 fl oz

solids

metric	imperial
20g	½ oz
60g	2 oz
125g	4 oz
180g	6 oz
250g	8 oz
500g	16 oz (1 lb)
1kg	32 oz (2 lb)

made to measure

equivalents for metric and
imperial measures and
ingredient names.

millimetres to inches

metric	imperial
3mm	⅛ inch
6mm	¼ inch
1cm	½ inch
2.5cm	1 inch
5cm	2 inches
18cm	7 inches
20cm	8 inches
23cm	9 inches
25cm	10 inches
30cm	12 inches

ingredient equivalents

bicarbonate soda	baking soda
capsicum	bell pepper
caster sugar	superfine sugar
celeriac	celery root
chickpeas	garbanzos
coriander	cilantro
cos lettuce	romaine lettuce
cornflour	cornstarch
eggplant	aubergine
green onion	scallion
plain flour	all-purpose flour
rocket	arugula
self-raising flour	self-rising flour
snow pea	mange tout
zucchini	courgette

oven temperature

setting the oven to the right temperature can be critical when making baked goods.

celsius to fahrenheit

celsius	fahrenheit
100°C	210°F
120°C	250°F
140°C	280°F
150°C	300°F
160°C	320°F
180°C	355°F
190°C	375°F
200°C	400°F
210°C	410°F
220°C	425°F

electric to gas

celsius	gas
110°C	¼
130°C	½
140°C	1
150°C	2
170°C	3
180°C	4
190°C	5
200°C	6
220°C	7
230°C	8
240°C	9
250°C	10

butter & eggs

let 'fresh is best' be your mantra when it comes to selecting dairy goods.

butter

For baking we generally use unsalted butter as it lends a sweeter flavour. Either way, the impact is minimal. One American stick of butter is 125g (4 oz).

eggs

Unless otherwise indicated we use large (60g) chicken eggs. To preserve freshness, store eggs in the refrigerator in the carton they are sold in. Use only the freshest eggs in recipes such as mayonnaise or dressings that use raw or barely cooked eggs. Be extra cautious if there is a salmonella problem in your community, particularly in food that is to be served to children, the elderly or pregnant women.

the basics

here are some simple weight conversions for cups of common ingredients.

common ingredients

almond meal (ground almonds)
1 cup : 120g
brown sugar
1 cup : 175g
white sugar
1 cup : 220g
caster (superfine) sugar
1 cup : 220g
icing (confectioner's) sugar
1 cup : 160g
plain (all-purpose)
or self-raising
(self-rising) flour
1 cup : 150g
fresh breadcrumbs
1 cup : 70g
finely grated parmesan cheese
1 cup : 80g
uncooked rice
1 cup : 200g
cooked rice
1 cup : 165g
uncooked couscous
1 cup : 200g
cooked, shredded chicken, pork or beef
1 cup : 160g
olives
1 cup : 150g

index

As well as listing all the recipes in the book by name alphabetically, there are multiple entries to help you find the recipe you want under its main ingredients, or according to its broader category or theme such as soups and salads, pasta, sauces and dressings. Whatever you're looking for, the information will be right at your fingertips.